The Lightweight Gourmet

*Drying and Cooking Food
for the Outdoor Life*

Alan S. Kesselheim
Illustrations by Marypat Zitzer

Ragged Mountain Press
Camden, Maine

To Donn and Chelsea,
who took us outdoors and fed
us well long before it
was fashionable

Published by Ragged Mountain Press

10 9 8 7 6 5 4 3

Copyright © 1994 Ragged Mountain Press,
a division of The McGraw-Hill Companies.

Library of Congress Cataloging-in-Publication Data
Kesselheim, Alan S., 1952–
    The lightweight gourmet: drying and cooking food for the outdoor
life / Alan S. Kesselheim.
        p.   cm.
    Includes bibliographical references and index.
    ISBN 0-07-034248-2
    1. Food—Drying.   2. Outdoor cookery.   3. Cookery (Dried foods)
4. Outdoor recreation—Equipment and supplies.   I. Title.
TX609.K47   1994
641.4'4—dc20   94-1332
                                                                      CIP

Questions regarding the content of this book should be addressed to:
Ragged Mountain Press
P.O. Box 220
Camden, ME   04843

Questions regarding the ordering of this book should be addressed to:
The McGraw-Hill Companies
Customer Service Department
P.O. Box 547
Blacklick, OH   43004
Retail Customers: 1-800-822-8158
Bookstores: 1-800-722-4726

A portion of the profits from the sale of each Ragged Mountain Press book is donated
to an environmental cause.

Printed by R. R. Donnelley, Crawfordsville, Indiana

Design by Edith Allard

Production by Dan Kirchoff

Edited by Jim Babb and Dorothy Chocensky

Contents

We start off in gray twilight. The sky is clear, boding well for the moonlight we're counting on to guide much of our climb. Our plan is to get above the loose, dangerous talus slope before darkness stops us, then wait for the full moon. The long ridge leading to the top of Mt. Lovinia will, we hope, be bathed in cool, pale light. We take sleeping bags and a little food, planning to sleep at the summit and catch sunrise hitting the high peaks of the Uinta Mountains.

The group is quiet, purposeful. We cross a high alpine meadow, then ascend a grassy slope to a small glacial lake. The steep talus rises above us, and we head into it at a steady pace as light wanes. Many of the rocks are tippy and precarious. We string out, work slowly, keep going. But darkness catches us with more talus ahead. We hunker at the base of a rock band to wait. It seems a long time. A few people nod off quietly while it grows very dark.

Finally the moon breaks above the horizon, sits astride the silhouettes of peaks and ridges. We stir, anticipating, but it is still a long wait for adequate light.

By the time we move again we're stiff and sleepy. Negotiating the talus is painfully slow, nerve-wracking. People talk in whispers, warning each other of loose rocks. Then the long ridge and a final steep pitch

*to the tiny peak. We all sit there then, in
silence, feeling our fatigue. The land too, a
vast dark spread of rumpled mountains and
distant plain, is quiet and at rest. Nothing
moves but the moon on its slow trail and,
now and then, a shooting star.*

*Sleeping bags come out. We all curl up in
the hollows between rocks, small flat places.
The clear air at 12,000 feet is cold and
sharp. It seems only a minute before the sky
brightens again and we rise to watch the
shadow of night retreat. All of us turn east
as if in a ritual ceremony, drawn irresistibly
to the first brilliant rays of the coming day.*

Introduction

This book is for people who love adventure and the outdoors; for people who want to be comfortable and at home
in the backcountry.

Adventure, too often, is associated with a spirit of con-
quest, with a kind of heroic athleticism most of us can't
relate to; and it is tainted by an elitist chauvinism that ex-
cludes *us*. Even common weekend outings are, frequently,
seen as survival tests—a few days of discomfort to endure
until we return to temperature-controlled environments,
pizza joints, and television.

For a long time I succumbed to that unfortunate state of
alienation during my outdoor jaunts. Much as I espoused
the wilderness lifestyle, much as I strove to live up to my

philosophy, I found it pretty tough going with my stomach growling uncomfortably and my thoughts wandering homeward.

Food plays a surprisingly important role in escaping from that state of discomfort, and in leaving behind the survive-the-wilds mentality.

Culinary fantasies used to be a routine element of campfire conversations. I endured dinners that all too quickly began to taste the same, expensive packets of "trail food" that yielded tiny, unsatisfying portions.

My attitudinal revolution occurred when I purchased a dehydrator and began to take charge of the food I ate on trips, the way I cooked, and the cost of my supplies. Twice now I have immersed myself on wilderness canoe journeys that have lasted more than a year at a stretch. I ate, on those trips, much as I do at home, and spent little more money than I normally would. My diet had variety, taste, nutrition, and the quantities I required.

Most important, my away-from-home existence has become comfortable. I no longer pine away for fast food, a pizza fix, or home-cooked meals. If I want a pizza, I make one. I eat home-cooked food every day. Instead of surviving the outdoor life, I embrace it and flourish in it.

If this sounds like what you aspire to, read on. Whether your outdoor ambitions take you on a year-long backpacking trek, a weekend camping trip, or a cycling tour of Europe, you'll find helpful material—drying charts for various foods, the equipment necessary for your wilderness kitchen, recipes and menu planners, even plans to build your own dehydrator. This information will transform your time on the trail from a rigorous, expensive ordeal into a pleasant, satisfying lifestyle; a lifestyle without walls or traffic jams, free of the hectic pace that has, more and more, come to be accepted as the normal way to live.

As you read, you'll encounter snippets of outdoor anecdote. Most have nothing to do with food, but everything to do with the well-fed contentment that leads to an appreciation for the power and serenity of wilderness; everything to do with the lure of adventure.

The Dry Life—Why Bother?

We have been windbound on this vast, cold lake for two days, so it is with exhilaration and relief that we finally paddle off. The waves are still large and scary, but the water calms as we paddle, and we don't stop until nearly dark. A tiny island offers us a one-tent campsite. We sit at its granite peak in a clearing, looking over the still water. The sky is aflame with sunset. Suddenly loons begin congregating in front of us. Five, eight, fifteen, finally twenty-six of the sleek, sharp-eyed birds swim nearby. They gabble at each other, seem to be discussing our arrival, then glide on past as night falls. Long after we lose sight of the loons, we hear their stirring talk coming through the northern twilight.

You Are the One in Charge
You tailor the menu, you select the foods, you develop the meals and nutritional balance to fit your travel style and appetites.

The Price Is Right
Entire dehydrated meals often cost less than a single component of a commercially packaged entree. I've been able to eat well and heartily for as little as three dollars a day.

Reduced Weight and Bulk
Anywhere from 50 to 90 percent of most food consists of water. As a result, dried meals can be reduced to a few ounces that fit in the palm of your hand. Using dehydrated food, I have canoed as long as 60 days without needing a resupply, and my boat has plenty of freeboard left. Dehydrated supplies fit easily in bicycle panniers, day packs, kayak hatches, or the cramped cupboards of a sailboat.

Tremendous Variety Is Yours
Vegetables, fruit, sauces, herbs and spices, even eggs and meat, can all be efficiently dried. Trip menus suddenly include quiche, enchilada casserole, curried rice and vegetables, eggs and hash browns; the possibilities go on and on.

Dry at Your Leisure
Stored properly, dried foods can last years. Put up food at any time. Garden produce, orchard pickings, wild game, sale items—it'll wait until you're ready to depart on the next adventure.

Meals Become a Satisfying Part of Backcountry Routine
In the survival-mentality style, meals are dispatched without ceremony or care. Dinner often amounts to dropping a plastic packet with a fancy label in boiling water, then wolfing down an amorphous glop. On the other hand, some of my most pleasant wilderness memories are set in camp, with my dinner simmering over the fire, the smells of savory food in the air, while a deep peaceful stillness or the sounds of calling loons and yipping coyotes fills the evening.

What It Takes to Start

It is -30°F on the March afternoon we
snowshoe into the Chipewyan winter camp.
Sled dogs whine and bark, a wall tent puffs
smoke, people come to greet us. Nearby, a
plastic-covered tepee houses a drying rack
draped with caribou meat. A smoldering fire
fills the tent with haze. It is soon dark, and
bitterly cold, but the wall tent full of people
is pleasantly cozy. Some of the "dry meat"
is pronounced done and brought in. The
natives spread lard on the meat like butter.
When I try it I am surprised by how good it
tastes. At the same time, we pass around
bags of our dried fruit, which is gobbled up
like candy.

Your Dehydrator

Preserving food by drying is as old as mankind. Laying
meat and berries out in the open air served people well for
thousands of years, and the technique still works. The
process can be as simple and rudimentary as hanging fish
in the sun, as the traditional Inuit people did, or laying
meat on a rack above a smoking fire.

I heard of a woman who dried fruit for her next outing
while she was off on the trail. She made sure to park her

car in the sun at the trail head, then placed trays of cut-up fruit on the shelf beneath the back window. By the time she returned, all she had to do was pop it into bags!

While the basic concept hasn't changed since early man, helpful appliances have multiplied dramatically. You can choose to start simply, as simply as using the sun or your oven, and evolve as necessary. There is no need to jump into a full-fledged food drying program, with all the hardware, until you're sure of your commitment.

If you're a builder, and want to be economical, consider constructing your own appliance (see "Two Easy Dehydrator Plans," page 78). A friend of mine made a dehydrator the size of a walk-in closet, capable of drying hundreds of pounds of produce at a whack.

I'm not a confident builder, and I figure that the years of design work that go into making an efficient, commercially marketed dehydrator are worth the expense.

Before you choose, ask yourself the following key questions: What are my needs? Will I use dehydrated food on weekend jaunts three times a year, or am I ambitious enough to require large quantities? As my needs expand, will the dehydrator's capacity easily expand as well? How energy efficient is the machine? How much of *my* time and energy will it require (rotating trays, turning trays, repairs, cleaning . . .)?

Low-Tech/No-Tech Options

Sun-drying
The original solar technology. Prepare food as for any dehydrator and lay it on screens. Place the screens at least 8 inches off the ground in direct sunlight (south-facing exposure) where air

can circulate freely around the food. Keep an eye out for insects, birds, and neighborhood pets. (Netting may be required.) Turn the food two or three times during the day. If the food isn't dry by nightfall, bring it inside to protect it from dew.

Oven-drying
Nothing wrong with using the same oven you bake in as a food dryer. The racks are already there, and you can use cookie sheets for liquids. Most ovens can be set as low as 140°F, which is a little too warm for fruits and veggies, but okay for liquids, meats, and dairy. Use an oven thermometer to check the setting. Prop the oven door open several inches to encourage some air circulation and moisture release, place the tray of food in the center, and you're in business.

Room-drying
Some things, such as herbs, chilis, snow peas, and green beans, will dry nicely if you simply hang them in the open air indoors. A fan to circulate air is helpful, but not essential.

Buying a Dryer
Over the long haul, the advantages of a store-bought dehydrator make the burden of its initial expense seem pretty puny. For $50 to $300 you can purchase a dehydrator with all the hardware to handle years of food processing, and bypass many of the shortcomings inherent with other methods.

Advantages of Commercial Dryers
- efficient airflow pattern powered by a fan
- exact temperature settings over a wide range
- even temperature distribution
- minimal need to rotate trays or turn food
- solid trays, mesh inserts, yogurt dishes, and other made-to-fit accessories
- fast drying without regard to weather
- energy savings—as little as three cents an hour to run

Shopping Tips

- A round design tends to ensure a more even airflow and temperature distribution.
- Check for the capability to expand drying capacity by adding trays.
- The walls and top should be insulated to minimize heat loss.
- Thermostat and fan are essential.
- Inquire about accessories for different drying tasks (solid inserts, quick-cleaning screens, jerky and yogurt makers, recipes and instructions, etc.).

American Harvest manufactures several circular models with a full line of accessories. Suggested retail ranges from $50 to $200. You can contact them at 4064 Peavey Road, Chaska, MN 55318, 800-624-2949.

Cus. 7/- 800-288-4545
ser.

Other Equipment

Food Processing Equipment

A good sharp paring knife is the only essential piece of equipment you'll need to ready produce for the dryer, but a few extra tools can be a godsend.

To begin with, try a *choy doh* (Chinese butcher knife). If you've ever been amazed by the dexterity and speed with which chefs at Chinese restaurants chop food, rest assured that a good deal of their skill is in the knife. The *choy doh* is the safest and fastest food processor this side of electricity.

My first years as a food dryer were made easier by the purchase of one of those primitive food aides with names like "Veg-O-Magic." You remember: "It slices! It dices!" It sounds silly, but that low-tech gadget slammed through a mountain of stuff. Alas, one tough carrot too many sounded its death knell, and I was back to the trusty paring knife.

Then I got married, and one of our wedding gifts was a terrifyingly efficient food processor. Our drying capacity took an astronomical leap. It's positively scary how quickly those things will render vegetables and fruit into helpless piles of shredded, sliced, or mashed food, ready to dry.

A blender can also be helpful for liquefying everything from tomato sauce to hummus to cooked apples, and it will help after drying when powdering dried eggs, tomato crystals, and so on.

Storage Containers
I like 5-gallon plastic buckets with snap-on lids. They are a good, workable size, are absolutely airtight, and keep food in darkness. Restaurants, university cafeterias, grocery stores, and food cooperatives are good sources for these, and you can often get them for a song.

Glass jars, big plastic bags, and cardboard barrels also work well. The important thing is to keep food sealed from light and air (see "Storage and Packaging," page 18).

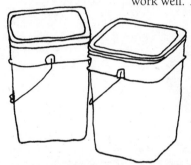

Bags and Heat Sealers
My technique is to double-bag everything in light-gauge plastic baggies, then store it in buckets. When I organize for a trip I invariably repack and reorganize my food. At that time I'll put individual meals into heavier-gauge, airlock bags.

Discount stores carry heat-sealing gizmos with heavy-mil rolls of plastic. You can custom-bag individual servings, entire meals, snacks, all as you please, and effectively seal out air.

Labels
It's startling how alike foods can look after the water is sucked out of them. To avoid the embarrassment of

standing around camp in near darkness, wondering if the tiny bag of green flakes you hold is spinach or cabbage or broccoli, it's good practice to identify and date each item as you bag it. The date is important, because you should use food that's been stored the longest first. If you don't want to get fancy, simply cut up scrap paper to make labels, or write the information directly on the bag with a freezer-wrap marker.

Mail Scale

A scale is optional, but some people are sticklers for details, and want to account for every ounce of pack weight. Also, your choice to dehydrate is constantly reaffirmed when you see how much food weight is nothing more than water. A scale that goes to 25 to 50 pounds is useful later on for weighing out entire meals or several days' food at once.

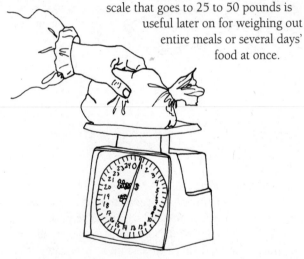

Your Provisions and What to Do with Them

Camp is set at the very edge of trees, surrounded by little clumps of wind-twisted spruce and stunted fir. The alpine valley is narrow and steep here, and jagged ridges of the San Juan Mountains loom over us. We are sleeping under a simple tarp strung between two short trees. As night comes on the air becomes heavy and stagnant; thunderheads cruise overhead like the black undersides of massive ships.

Then it is dark, quickly and utterly dark. We huddle together beneath the flimsy layer of nylon like animals in a burrow. When the storm hits it is without prelude. Suddenly the valley is lit with stabbing platinum light. Thunder rocks the amphitheater of ancient stone. Again and again I see momentary flashes of crags and pinnacles, trees waving in the wind, our packs leaned together, then am plunged into pitch darkness, waiting for the blow of sound to follow. Rain pummels the tarp just above my head; wind snaps the fabric. Oddly, it is not fear or anxiety I feel, but heart-pounding exhilaration. What I feel, at the core, is very alive.

Within hours of getting my food dehydrator home, I had the trays laden with their first batch of fruit and vegetables. I couldn't resist peeking to see what apples looked like as they lost moisture, or to discover whether cabbage would actually disappear by the time it dried. There is something satisfying and miraculous about this metamorphosis, changing food into such a reduced, withered form; food that will wait patiently for the moment you choose to return it, again miraculously, to its original state.

Food Sources

From the start I had an eye out for cheap sources of food and for opportunities to gather supplies in bulk. Most of us buzz off to the store once a week or so and buy a quantity of perishables that we can use up before they go bad. A dehydrator grants you the freedom to indulge in bulk, to take advantage of foods that are in season or on sale, and to dry at the peak of freshness.

When peaches are cheap, lug home a 30-pound box instead of 3 or 4 for your fruit bowl. When green peppers are 8 for a dollar, get 50! In a matter of a day or two, depending on your drying capacity, they'll be safely preserved.

Farmer's markets and fruit stands are terrific sources of fresh, unpackaged produce. Orchards often have seasonal specials or pick-your-own deals. I've found apple trees in my neighborhood that are never harvested. People are usually happy to let me pick, and the tart flavor of the small, wild apples makes for wonderful dried fruit.

Your own garden can provide good quantities of vegetables and herbs/spices. Instead of canning or freezing your excess garden produce, try drying it. Seed catalogs and gardening books will sometimes note which varieties dry well.

If you're drying for a big adventure—sailing around the world, say, or hiking the Appalachian Trail—talk to your local grocers about produce that is still good, but not adequate for display. There is usually a back room somewhere housing a treasure trove of food that might otherwise go to waste. If you find friends there who are captured by the excitement of your endeavor, they'll lead you to quantities of free and discounted fruits and vegetables. At the very least, store owners will usually let you buy at case lot or bulk prices.

For big projects, don't limit yourself to fresh food alone. Some canned or frozen products dry well, cost very little, and add variety to your stock. Canned green chilis dry up until they're nearly weightless and add character to enchiladas or chili. Canned tomato sauce is easily dried, as are refried beans, bottled salsa, frozen vegetables, canned pineapple. While you lose some of the goodness of fresh products, canned and frozen foods are easy to prepare (usually nothing more than zipping a can open and dumping it on a tray), and you can take advantage of weekly specials to further reduce your trip expense. Besides, many foods available in frozen or canned form are rarely available fresh.

The Prep

Fruit

Fruits are almost all ready to dry without much treatment. Wash them well, core or pit apples, pears, peaches, and the like, cut away any bruised areas, and you're ready to go. For best results slice fruit uniformly, so it'll all be done at once. Small fruits like cherries can be cut in half, or even dried whole after you crack or pierce the skin. Larger fruits should be sliced evenly, but not too thin, or they'll come out like communion wafers.

Skinning fruit is a matter of personal preference. Without skins the drying goes more quickly and evenly, but it involves more prep work and some people prefer the tangy flavor of skins. Try it both ways to see which camp you're in. To dry

Fruit Pretreatment Methods

Some people are put off by the browning that naturally occurs in the drying of fruits. Although it isn't necessary to treat any fruit before drying, there are some simple methods for those that prefer the look of unbrowned fruit.

Salt Solution: Soak prepared fruit for no more than 5 minutes, before putting on trays, in a saltwater solution of 2 quarts water to 3 tablespoons salt.

Vitamin C Bath: Dissolve 2 tablespoons vitamin C crystals or powder (10, 500-mg. tablets) in 1 quart warm water and let prepared fruit soak for 5 minutes.

Lemon Juice Soak: Use ¼ cup lemon juice for every quart of warm water and let prepared fruit sit in the solution for 5 minutes.

There are a number of more involved pretreatment procedures, but most, like sulfuring, syrup blanching, sulfur/steaming, are quite elaborate and time-consuming.

---

apricots or other halved fruit, lay them skin-side down on the trays to better retain flavor. Check the drying charts (beginning on page 37) for temperature.

Fruit will generally turn brown as it dries. To minimize browning and loss of vitamins, dry at the peak of ripeness and as soon as possible after preparation. Dry each batch steadily and without interruption at a constant heat.

Fresh Vegetables

As with fruit, select vegetables at their peak, wash them in cold water, and cut away bruises. Peel or pare the tough, fibrous sections, and core if necessary (outer sheath of broccoli, outside leaves of cabbage heads, innards of green peppers). Slice, shred, or chop vegetables uniformly to suit your recipes.

Almost all vegetables require a pretreatment step to

retard the enzyme action that can eventually lead to spoilage. Only a few varieties, such as mushrooms, tomatoes, and onions, escape this fate. The easiest method of treatment is water or steam blanching (steam retains more of the water-soluble vitamins and minerals). Use a double boiler or steamer insert, and pile the vegetables loosely no more than 2 to 3 inches deep. Steam until heated through and slightly tender (not fully cooked). Stir contents periodically, if necessary, to steam evenly.

Meat and Dairy

High fat content in meat and dairy products make them the trickiest of the food groups to dry and store. The general rule is to handle them as little as possible, dry them quickly, and use them up before prolonged storage permits them to go rancid.

The most common use for dehydrated meat is jerky, for which beef or game meat works best. Smoked fish is popular as well. (See recipes on pages 52–53.)

Beef, game, and poultry can also be dried to add to stews, soups, chilis, and other field dishes. Prepare by cooking thoroughly (usually by boiling), then allow to cool. Pick off or cut away any remaining fat. Chop into cubes, shred, or grind up, and dry until all discernible moisture has been removed. Avoid uncooked pork products, because even high-temperature drying won't completely assure the destruction of trichinella parasites.

For vegetarians or those who remain leery of dried meats, tofu (soybean curd) is a viable substitute. Try to get firm tofu cakes. Butcher it into 1-inch cubes or thin strips, and dry without any treatment. Add to stews and soups in the field (it will take on the flavor of the dish), or steep in a marinade (see jerky recipes on pages 52–53) for preflavored chunks, which can be eaten as is or added to the pot.

Eggs are the main dairy product worth the trouble of drying. Again, high fat content is a concern, so minimize the time spent handling and processing. Break the desired number of raw eggs into a bowl (I do eight on a tray) and beat them together. Add spices if you'd like before pouring onto the tray insert. Set at fairly high heat (140°F) until the surface is dry and crumbly to the touch.

Grated cheese can be dried for good snacks. Powdered cheese is available too, but I've never been satisfied with it for cooking. There is no substitute for the real stuff in the field, however, and cheese is one of the few foods I carry fresh into the backcountry.

Canned and Frozen Food

Canned foods—from green beans to refried beans, pineapple to green chilis—are as simple to dry as one could ever ask. Open the can, drain out liquid, dash the contents evenly onto your trays, and fire up your

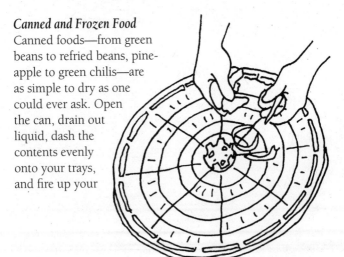

dehydrator. Use the drying charts (beginning on page 37) as a guide, although times for processed food will differ somewhat from fresh.

Frozen foods are almost as easy. I usually steam-blanch frozen vegetables slightly, both to thaw them and to retard any stubborn enzyme activity, then get on with it.

Liquids

Fruit leathers, leftover spaghetti sauce, eggs, tomato sauce, stews, hummus, all require containment. Most store-bought dehydrators come with tray or shelf inserts for this purpose. If you opt for a homemade dryer, you'll need to customize your own plastic sheets, or use a plastic wrap or waxed paper layer to contain the fluid.

To dry liquids quickly, spread the layer fairly thin (less than ½ inch deep). Trays will often dry more rapidly in some sections than in others (depending on the pattern of air flow). Once you identify the tendency, concentrate food more thickly where it dries faster.

Blend or puree the food so it's a fairly consistent thickness. Big chunks won't dry at the same rate as sauce, resulting in pockets of moisture. If, in the case of leftovers, you want to retain the chunkiness of a dish, strike a balance between overdrying some of it and underdrying the rest. Once packaged, the moisture will distribute itself throughout the contents.

Precooked Staples

Much of your cooking time in the field is devoted to simmering rice, beans, pasta, or some other staple ingredient. For the most part I don't begrudge that time, but there are instances when fuel is limited or you simply need to get a meal into your bowl fast. If you cook and dry staples at home, quick meals on the trail can be routine.

Beans

Pinto, Anasazi, kidney, or other dried beans should be soaked overnight and then cooked until tender (1 to 2 hours). Rinse beans thoroughly and add a bit of salt (optional) for flavor. Dry whole, mash into pieces (a potato-masher works well), or coarsely puree in a blender or food processor. Dry at 135°F until hard (3 to 10 hours). To rehydrate, cover beans with water (hot water works best) for 1 hour or more before meal time, or simmer gently, adding more water as needed. If you simmer too long, the beans will start to disintegrate.

Rice
Cook brown or white basmati rice until tender, then spread on solid trays. Try to avoid big clumps. Dry at 135°F until hard (2 to 6 hours). Put the rice in a plastic bag and work it between your fingers to break it apart. Rehydrate by soaking in water before meal time or recooking it with twice as much water as rice. Cooking time will be about half the usual.

Pasta
Cook pasta in plenty of boiling water, rinse, then spread on trays. Dry at 135°F for 2 to 6 hours, until noodles are brittle and hard. Soak in warm water to rehydrate, or boil noodles for about half the normal cooking time.

Not Worth the Effort
After years at this game, I've come to the conclusion that there are a few foods that simply aren't worth the effort to dry. Take onions, for instance. The first time we took on those little devils we brought home a 50-pound sack, chuckling all the way over our great savings. A week later we finally finished the last one off, having endured the indignities of various home cures for tearing eyes, and vowing never to dry another bloody onion as long as we lived. At one point that week, near midnight, we looked at each other over the pile of onion skins and collapsed in hysterics. Each of us wore a pair of ski goggles and a bandanna, bandit style, and had a piece of white bread stuffed in our mouth. None of it worked, so don't bother. Ever since then, we've found diced onion bits at very reasonable prices through our local health-food store.

Dried potatoes are also cheap and readily available, and save you the chopping, blanching chore. Powdered milk is expensive, but worth the price. You may find other dried products in your area stores that will be worth the laborsaving convenience.

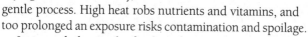

Into the Heat

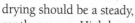

You've done the hard part. Now it's time to zap food into the dry dimension. Remember, drying should be a steady, gentle process. High heat robs nutrients and vitamins, and too prolonged an exposure risks contamination and spoilage.

In general, dry similar foods at the same time to minimize mixing of flavors and odors. I've mixed a variety of fruits or several kinds of vegetables in the same load without trouble, but some foods have a very pervasive quality and are best dried alone—green peppers, for instance, and mushrooms. Load the trays evenly, with space between pieces so the air flow is free to contact all parts of the food. With time you'll develop speed-loading techniques—sprinkling some things, pouring on liquids with a flourish of the wrist, dealing out pineapple slices like a Las Vegas pro.

Becoming accustomed to a dryer is like working into the idiosyncrasies of a new backpack or discovering the quirks of a strange boat. Every machine is unique. Before you get to know your drying unit, check frequently to see if trays need rotating, or if food should be moved around on the same layer. Use the drying charts as a guideline, but understand that altitude, climate, fluctuations in the amount of food in a batch, variations in dehydrators, and other factors will shorten or lengthen those times.

Testing for doneness is an acquired skill, more a matter of experience and feel than of hard and fast rules. When food is nearly ready, remove a piece and allow it to cool.

Fruits should be leathery, with a chewy texture, and free of obvious moisture pockets. Vegetables should have less moisture remaining than fruit, so they'll often feel brittle and crisp. Meat and dairy products need to be quite free of moisture. When they're done, they'll be crumbly, flaky, very dry to the touch. (Beef jerky will be more pliable.)

Don't overdry foods. If you do, you run the risk of losing nutrients, making food tough, and turning your hard-earned provisions into tasteless chips. With practice you'll have the sense of timing down, just like a good cook knows the perfect moment to serve a meal.

Storage and Packaging

The enemies of dried food are sunlight, air, moisture, and high temperatures. The ideal storage site, therefore, is cool, dark, and dry. Airtight food containers are a must.

As soon as possible after drying, place foods in sealed bags or containers. Try to divide it up into meal-size or one-day amounts to minimize repeated exposure to air. Use double bags, freezer-lock bags, or heat-sealed vacuum bags, labeled with both date and contents.

If you're drying significant quantities of supplies, organize them by general category and store in airtight containers. Cardboard barrels, 5-gallon plastic buckets with lids, or sealed glass jars will all work.

Keep your dried food stockpiled in a cool, dark corner of the basement or at the back of a closet. Meats and eggs should, if possible, be kept in a freezer until you depart. For every 10°F you lower the storage environment, the shelf life increases by months.

Every so often, rummage through your bags. Too much retained moisture in foods will manifest itself eventually in mold, and those bags should be discarded.

Once in the field, maintain the essential airless, lightless, low-temperature conditions as best you can, and pack so that you avoid opening and reopening bags.

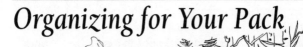

Organizing for Your Pack

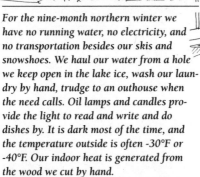

For the nine-month northern winter we have no running water, no electricity, and no transportation besides our skis and snowshoes. We haul our water from a hole we keep open in the lake ice, wash our laundry by hand, trudge to an outhouse when the need calls. Oil lamps and candles provide the light to read and write and do dishes by. It is dark most of the time, and the temperature outside is often -30°F or -40°F. Our indoor heat is generated from the wood we cut by hand.

"How harsh!" people say when they hear about our winters in the Canadian north. "I could never do that!"

But think what we have freed ourselves from. We have no vehicle to pamper and struggle with on those cold mornings. No pipes will freeze at our place. There is no job we must get to, no groceries to shop for, no day care or banking or health club workout or any of the rest that we clutter our civilized lives with.

If it's really bad outside, if the winds howl and the storms rage, we just stay at home, throw more wood in the stove, and watch the drama. When it ends we have the silence, the weaving northern lights, the birds and animals that share our neighborhood. And we have time to savor it all.

By far the most trying and difficult part of any trip comes before you leave home. Days, weeks, and sometimes even years make up the thankless drudgery prerequisite to any major journey—packing, preparing food, going down endless lists, saving money, coping with logistics and pretrip group dynamics. If you have the stamina and fortitude to withstand that, the challenges of your adventure will be a cakewalk.

Drudgery it may be, but that prep period is time well spent. Shortcuts will inevitably come back to haunt you. If you just throw everything together helter-skelter and head off, you'll pay for your haste again and again. It is no time to confront the chaos of an unorganized food pack when you're under attack by insects, or threatened by an impending storm, or making camp after dark. Do it once, before you leave, and you'll forget the hassles as soon as you lose sight of civilization.

Convenience in Packaging

Think through the process of meal preparation, and package your food to minimize steps in the field:

- mix the powdered milk in with cold cereal so all you have to do is add water
- prebag the bannock (camp bread) ingredients in one-batch amounts
- dry the breakfast eggs with the desired spices already added
- don't bother separating things into different bags if they will cook together (beans and dried veggies, for instance)
- cut and wrap cheese in convenient amounts (½-pound chunks work pretty well)
- bag food in one-meal quantities when possible (especially important for dried foods, since repeated exposure to air can lead to spoilage)

Color-coded Stuff Sacks

I make four piles of my trip food: breakfast, lunch, dinner, and pantry. Each pile then goes into stuff sacks of all the same color. Breakfast will be blue, lunch maroon, dinner silver, and so on. When you're looking for that elusive bottle of oil, you'll at least know which colored bag to grab.

If you don't have an array of colored sacks to choose from, mark bags with colored tape, magic marker, or thread to accomplish the same end. As I place the food bags in packs I try to keep all the sacks of each color together so that as a trip goes on, I won't have to suffer through an endless repetition of the search-and-discover process.

Some people get so organized that they have each day's food bagged in a separate sack and marked with its designated number in the trip itinerary. I prefer the flexibility to pick and choose meals based on the day's character.

Handy Utensils

As with your food, keep cooking utensils in accessible and centralized spots. On canoe trips I usually designate one pack as the equipment mule, in which I'll keep the pots, pans, grill, stove, fuel, and other cookwear. For backpacking or biking, the pot set should be in a compact, easy-to-grab nest. Stove and utensils should also be in a handy bag or bags near the top of your load. Matches or lighters shouldn't be kept with the pots, as they tend to be wet. I try to have several waterproofed bags of matches scattered in different places, and a lighter for backup.

When I reach camp, it's a comfort to know which bag to

grab for dinner and where to locate the cookset, and to have matches in hand. Likewise, in the morning, I like to know exactly where the coffee and my mug are stashed!

Packing for the Day

Every morning, or even the night before, get all your lunch stuff together and store it in a specific, accessible place. I use a fanny pack clipped to a canoe thwart on boat trips, but any small stuff sack or dry bag will work. Pack it near the top of your pack, bike pannier, or kayak hatch. When lunch rolls around, there's no rooting through cavernous packs for cheese and trail mix. Any morale-boosting treats, drink crystals, or commonly used condiments can go in the same place. Make sure a water bottle is somewhere in reach, and that your pocket knife is either in your pocket or stowed conveniently.

Expect the Worst

Assume that when you get to camp it will be dark, raining hard, and hellish with bugs. When you think that way, the cooking tarp will always be right at the top of your pack, pannier, or dry bag, with the guy strings neatly wrapped. When the worst happens, set up your tarp, gather your belongings around you, and regroup. Once under the protective eaves, it's your choice whether to light a stove or kindle a fire for hot drinks. Hot drinks, by the way, are always the first step toward achieving a calm state of mind.

Your flashlight, bug dope, and matches should also be easy to grab, ready for the bad day that comes at least once every trip.

Along that line, it isn't a bad idea to stow away a bag of fire-starter (curls of birch bark, wood chips, little dry spruce twigs) somewhere in a pack to get that critical blaze going when hypothermia comes knocking.

Odds and Ends

As a trip goes on, designate a spare stuff sack to hold the inevitable accumulation of leftover uncooked bits of food that pile up. This can serve as a kind of reserve pantry supply and an extra stash if food runs low. I've had some very interesting meals when a trip went a day longer than planned, and dinner was concocted from an assortment of this and that dried veggie, a soup mix, a quarter cup of rice left over in a bag, and a hunk of cheese. Add generous amounts of Cajun spice, a healthy quotient of fatigue, and mystery dinners taste pretty wonderful!

Containers

Appropriately sized, leakproof containers are worth their weight in gourmet popcorn! There's nothing quite like a leaky honey container in the middle of your pack to ruin a nice day in the bush. Oil, tamari, hot sauce, margarine—all of them have potential for inside-the-pack toxic spills.

Round, wide-mouth plastic containers with stout, screw-top lids work well for peanut butter, jam, bulk margarine, or butter. Small-mouth bottles in 1-pint size work best for tamari, oil, and that sort of thing. Small plastic bowls or sandwich containers with snap-on lids aren't dependable enough to carry liquids for weeks at a stretch, but they do nicely for reconstituting and carrying the day's dried hummus or lentil pâté in the lunch sack. Labeled film canisters or tamper-proof prescription bottles are good spice containers. Whatever the vessel, try not to have lots of extra space inside. That air you carry around in bottles and jars takes up room that more important stuff could fill.

The old food tubes we all used to carry around are only marginally adequate. The clip closures tend to crack and break, it's easy to lose the lids, and they're a struggle to clean. About the only thing I ever use them for is reconstituting salsa, and even at that, I make sure to have spare lids and closures in the repair kit.

There are several new-generation plastics that manufacturers claim will not take on the taste, smell, and residue of their contents. Lexan, for one, works pretty well, although a few weeks at a stretch carrying tamari or olive oil might be a match for any plastic. I now have an assortment of bottles permeated with the telltale odor of their usual trip contents. "Yup," I'll say, after one whiff, "this one's for the tamari."

The Outdoor Kitchen

This is the problem. Our route requires us to find a way over the massive desert mesa that squats between two major canyons. If we don't, our itinerary is a bust and we have to retrace thirty miles of dusty trail. We enter hopefully at every side canyon, go far enough up to see the sandstone walls leading upward to the piñon and juniper flats at the top, and search with binoculars for likely breaks. There have been none. Time after time the sandstone rises sheer for a thousand feet, or overhangs impossibly, or the promising benches peter out in thin air.

Mile after mile that we will have to repeat if we fail drops behind us, until we come to the final draw, our last hope. A ways in there is a friction slope that gains us the first stage of altitude, followed by a gentle curve of cross-bedded sandstone, and then a sheer wall. We scout gingerly along a shelf at its base, sometimes on a bench as wide as a sidewalk, sometimes on a ledge barely the width of our boots. At every tough spot we ask ourselves whether we could return if we hit a dead end.

Then there's an eroded gully in the rock with a lip at chest height. We can't see above it, but it is the most promising spot yet. Up we scramble. A steep narrow cleft confronts us almost immediately. We discuss it at length, then brace ourselves in the

chimney of rock and go up. I try not to think of coming back down.

But it is the crux. Above us is an expanse of easy friction rock, and we almost jog up it in excitement to a final band of cliff and we quickly find a route through to the top.

Below us spread the snaking dry canyons, the sheer walls, and, in the distance, the snowy high peaks. White-throated swifts chatter and dive beneath our feet, charging through the air with what seems like reckless, giddy delight.

We camp there, a dry camp in the shelter of a spreading piñon pine. It is good to be on top, to see the sunset across one hundred miles of canyon desert, to smell the sap of pine, and to remember the success of our climb. In the morning we will try to find our way down the other side.

Some people eat the same way they fill up the gas tank of their car. Simple refueling, and the faster the better. This chapter—this entire book, for that matter—is not for them. It's likely that at home they do most of their cooking in the microwave, or by dialing the phone for take-out.

I enjoy cooking at home. I find the smell of simmering spaghetti sauce comforting and satisfying. I like to know what I'm eating, and to participate in the creation of nutritious and tasteful meals. That isn't to say that a fast dinner isn't required at times, or that daily events don't sometimes preclude dawdling over the stew pot. Knowing how to whip up a quick entree is a valuable skill, too. But preparing and eating food should be a pleasant and relaxing, if routine, part of each day, whether in the confines of suburbia or in the midst of a great blank space on the map.

Perhaps the most important factor in achieving that enjoyment is knowing your kitchen and feeling comfortable and competent there. Having the right tools handy and the food organized sensibly, and being at ease in your cooking space, are the first ingredients of successful meals.

The same holds true in the wilderness, on a sailboat, along a bicycle route, or wherever the trail takes you. Allow yourself the luxury of enjoying the food that is your fuel, of taking the time to prepare good, hearty meals. Those times in camp while dinner is baking in the Dutch oven or coffee is perking in the pot can be some of the most rewarding interludes in your journey. Time to discuss the day's events, study maps, play a round of cribbage, jot notes in your journal. Time to be still and let the surroundings sink in.

Stoves Versus Fires

Traditional camp scenes were pungent with wood smoke. The sounds of a crackling fire and kindling being chopped were the auditory background. The stew pot hung from a wire or rested on a metal grill set above the fire, and after dinner the flames warmed the group as stars appeared and the night noises in the forest came alive.

Modern camps, on the other hand, are tinged with the smell of gasoline. The roar of a compact stove drowns out conversation or hisses insistently under the pot. A shiny kettle rests over the even blue flame pumped out of a pressurized fuel canister.

You can tell by my descriptions, perhaps, where my bias lies, but there are reasonable arguments, and reasonable environments, for both camping styles. I am equally at home in either kitchen. Your destination, mode of travel, and personal preference will dictate which is most appropriate on a given journey.

Conditions Conducive to Fires

- plentiful down and dead wood
- ability to carry bulkier cookware
- environment in which fire scars can be cleaned up or a fire pan used
- menu that includes baking and requires the capability to cook several things simultaneously on one fire

Conditions Conducive to Stoves

- lack of wood, due either to environmental circumstances or to human pressure on an area

- heavily traveled area where fire scars cannot be cleaned up and harvesting available wood is inappropriate
- need to strictly limit weight and bulk in your pack
- simple, one-pot meals

Cleaning Up

The major arguments against using wood fires hang on the environmental impact of consuming available wood and the problem of leaving campfire scars behind. In parts of the world where fuel is scarce and/or human traffic heavy, that argument is compelling. We've all seen the effects of careless abuse and uninhibited overuse.

Stoves are clean to start with, the argument goes, and leave no scars behind. In a limited sense that's true. But don't forget that the fuel that powers stoves is produced by extractive, environmentally damaging industries, and that the manufacture of stoves has an impact on the environment.

If we use wilderness areas, we have a responsibility to pass them on to the next traveler in the same, or improved, condition. That caveat, along with a commonsense evaluation, should dictate your actions.

If you decide on fires, follow these guidelines:

- Use only down and dead wood or driftwood, and be sensitive to overuse in environments that take many years to regenerate tree growth (desert, alpine, tundra).
- If you have the room, carry a simple fire pan (even the lid of a metal trashcan works) to eliminate fire scars.
- Build your fires in places where the scars can be cleaned up (beaches, below the high watermark on rivers, in gravel).
- When making fires in a vegetated area, cut out a small piece of sod with a trowel and remove it intact to replace when you're finished.
- Build fires small—a roaring blaze isn't necessary or efficient for cooking food.
- If a fire scar already exists at a site, use it instead of creating a fresh one, then do your best to clean it up.
- Burn wood completely and scatter or bury the ashes.

"Zip" Stoves

For an alternative to stoves powered by gasoline or fuel canisters, consider the Sierra stove. It consumes the most unlikely, inauspicious fuel—pine cones, wood chips, general forest litter, even dry moose turds. The stove requires a battery, which will last roughly a week of normal cooking. Carry rechargeables and a small solar battery charger for the long haul. They burn surprisingly hot.

In the final analysis, your choice of fire or stove should be based on your cooking preferences weighed against a sensitive assessment of environmental impact. Most of the recipes in this book can be prepared on stoves or fires. The few that require baking under coals are so indicated.

Critters

I almost didn't include this topic, because, in my opinion, it's a nonissue that has been dutifully sensationalized for decades in book after book. I have camped in thousands of sites and in almost every environment, yet can count on one hand the times I've been inconvenienced by critters. Beyond that, most of those instances occurred in quasi-civilized campgrounds where critters, naturally, made the most of a good thing.

Outdoor books almost all include the obligatory sketch

of good campers hanging their food sack in a handy tree. Hogwash! Good food-hanging trees are about as common as wild condors, even in a mature forest. In high alpine, desert, or tundra environments you're flat out of luck. Even if you do find that perfect tree, don't believe the three-step diagram in whatever book you use. It will take half the evening to effectively hang your weighty sack well out of reach of a motivated bear. Last time I checked, bears were a good deal more agile and powerful than humans. Anyway, it doesn't work.

Bears and other food scavengers are attracted by smell, or they make routine rounds of well-used sites. Hanging food doesn't remove odors, so the animals will still come to your camp and keep you awake and cowering with their trapeze exploits.

Far better to remove the odor and remove temptation. Keep a clean camp and take care of your trash. Store food in double plastic bags, Ziploc bags, or plastic barrels with screw tops made specifically for camping. In Denali National Park odorproof plastic food barrels are mandatory backcountry equipment and bear/people hassles have been cut to almost nil.

Sleep well away from your cooking area and food, and pack everything up securely before retiring. Try to avoid camping in the same spot night after night. Beyond that, you might try some odor distractions around your food packs. Open vials of ammonia, moth balls, and bug dope are rumored to be effective.

The Nomadic Kitchen

Remember, comfort and efficiency are the watchwords. Your kitchen needs to operate smoothly in rain and heat, in snow and cold, and in whatever location is home for the night. A few key techniques and pieces of equipment go a long way toward ensuring that.

A Comfortable Cooking Area

The cook requires convenient access to the supplies that make up dinner and the pots that need stirring and tending.

Gather the appropriate color-coded bags around you before you start, along with the spice kit, the hot drinks, and so on. If your stove sits on the ground, a collapsible padded camp chair is nice to sit in and offers the benefit of a back-rest. If dinner is cooking on top of a grill or perched on a higher rock, a bit more elevation is handy. I usually sit on the waterproof ammo can that keeps my camera gear dry. It's hard and lacks a backrest, but I'm moving around enough that I wouldn't be reclining anyway. When it comes time to eat and relax I move into the camp chair and lean back to enjoy.

A convenient boulder can raise your cooking platform to the same level as your counters and stove at home, allowing you to stand and stir. Likewise, if you're winter camping in deep snow, dig out a kitchen with customized shelving and counter space.

The Cook Tarp

Few things are worse than making dinner in a steady rain or under relentless sunlight. Cooking inside the cramped confines of your tent is little better. A small tarp weighs

next to nothing, can be rigged in minutes, and provides shelter from the elements while you perform your culinary wizardry.

I prefer a slanting tarp with the high end facing away from the wind and the low end still several feet off the ground. Packs and gear can stay dry at the back, people can stand comfortably at the front, and water drains efficiently off the slope of nylon.

Build your fire just out from the front of the tarp, or fire up the stove just inside the eaves. A 10-foot-by-12-foot nylon tarp with cord in the grommets is adequate for two to four people.

If trees aren't handy, you'll find out how resourceful you are with bicycle frames, kayak paddles, driftwood sticks, or nearby boulders.

There are several models of pyramid-shaped shelters with a single, telescoping center pole. These offer a quick and comfy cooking space for stoves. They aren't cheap, but they are handy.

A Prep Surface

Ever minced an onion in the palm of your hand, or diced cheese in a tiny bowl? If you have, you know the value of a nice, flat surface. Some people I know go to the extreme of toting along a wooden cutting board, but it's cumbersome and heavy. A thin hard-plastic cutting board works best. The lid of a pot or the broad side of an ammo can can fill the bill in a pinch. Traditional canoeists who still carry a wannigan (a wooden box for cook gear) have their traveling kitchen counter with them in the wilderness. The rest of us have to make do.

Kitchen Equipment List

The following list supplies a very complete expedition kitchen. Adapt as required for shorter, lighter, or more civilized jaunts.

Basic Supplies

- cup/bowl/spoon for each trip member
- waterproof matchsafes and lighter
- pocket knife (after losing several camp knives, sometimes where I could least afford it, I've taken to tying my knife to my belt loop with a length of cord)
- cooking tarp (10 feet by 12 feet)
- water containers (a 2½-gallon collapsible jug folds down to nothing and keeps you from jogging to the water source every time you need to fill a pot)

- small, plastic cutting board
- pot lifters (a bandanna does in a pinch, but light pliers or grippers made for this purpose are infinitely better)
- scrubby sponge
- biodegradable soap
- 2-quart pot
- wooden spoon
- small spatula
- fillet knife (if fresh fish is on the menu)
- coffee filter that doesn't require paper inserts (several models are available—try tea and coffee shops)

If You Opt for Fires

- folding grill
- hatchet and/or folding saw
- small trowel (for moving coals and preparing the fire site)
- cast aluminum Dutch oven (lighter than you think—10- to 12-inch-diameter feeds two to four people)
- small cast aluminum griddle with lip (or fry pan)
- stuff sacks for pots to keep fire soot from dirtying your pack

If You Opt for Stoves
- backpacking stove
- fuel bottles and pour spout or funnel
- fry pan with lid
- large (1 gallon) cooking pot

Dutch ovens may seem like equipment from the days of voyageurs and wagon trains, but they are an extremely versatile and useful piece of wilderness kitchen gear. They double as a general pot, can be found in lightweight cast aluminum, and will cook everything from coq au vin to apple pie.

Drying Times

It's mid-February in the mountains of
Montana, nearly dark, and we've admitted
to being lost. The snow is so deep that the
trail blazes on trees are covered up. For a
time we followed the gap the trail-cut made
through the forest, but the trees are thick,
and somewhere we must have veered off.

Every so often we ski to a likely looking
tree and dig away snow in hopes of
uncovering a blaze, but with no luck. The
four of us huddle up around the map again
and again, trying to interpret the lay of the
land. We aim the compass here and there,
build our cases for being in this spot or that.

But now it's more important to find a
sheltered spot to camp and get some food
going than it is to regain the trail. We
descend to a small saddle in the ridge,
burrow into a thicket of spruce, shed our
packs.

Before long our kitchen has been dug out
of the snow, a room with benches, shelves,
cupboards. A room that will evaporate come

> *spring. The stove roars reassuringly on its*
> *ledge. Mugs of hot chocolate soon warm our*
> *hands. The stars are thick in the black-ice*
> *sky, glittering through the branches of*
> *spruce. We're not really lost. It feels*
> *remarkably like a home right here. The trail*
> *mystery can wait.*

The temperatures and times below are based on using a store-bought, thermostatically controlled dehydrator. Times for sun-drying, light-bulb dehydrators, and other drying methods will vary. For foods not listed, try to find an item of comparable texture and consistency.

Food	Prep/Treatment	Temp/Time	Doneness Test
Fruit	*(All fruits dry at 135°F)*		
Apples	Core; slice ½" thick	6–14 hrs.	Leathery
Apricots	Pit; slice in half	8–20 hrs.	Leathery
Bananas	Peel; slice ⅛"–¼" thick, or separate lengthwise in 3 natural divisions	5–24 hrs.	Hard chips or somewhat pliable strips
Berries	If small, dry whole; slice larger varieties; boil wax-covered berries 2 mins. to break skin	4–20 hrs.	Leathery or hard, depending on type
Cherries	Pit; halve; place skin-side down on tray	8–20 hrs.	Leathery, tacky
Cranberries	Boil 2 mins.; halve, or dry whole	5–15 hrs.	Leathery
Grapes	Boil 1 min.; dry whole	8–20 hrs.	Leathery
Fruit Leather	Spread up to ½" thick	8–20 hrs.	Pliable, often sticky
Kiwis	Cut ends; peel; slice ¼"–⅜" thick	8–12 hrs.	Slightly pliable, sticky
Oranges	Don't peel; slice ½" thick; powder when dry for cooking uses	8–16 hrs.	Hard, crisp

Fruit	*(All fruits dry at 135°F)*		
Peaches	Pit; slice ½" thick	8–16 hrs.	Leathery
Pears	Core; slice ½" thick	8–16 hrs.	Leathery
Pineapple	Core; peel; slice ¼"–⅜" thick	8–20 hrs.	Leathery, sticky
Plums	Pit; halve, or slice ½" thick	8–20 hrs.	Leathery
Rhubarb	Chop in 1" pieces	4–12 hrs.	Leathery

Vegetables	*(All veggies dry at 130°F)*		
Asparagus	Dry in spears or cut in 1" lengths	6–12 hrs.	Brittle
Beans (Green or Wax)	Steam until softened; dry whole or in pieces	6–12 hrs.	Brittle
Beets	Steam or boil until done; peel; slice ¼" thick	8–12 hrs.	Brittle
Broccoli	Trim fibrous sheath; chop, or cut in thin strips; steam until nearly done	8–12 hrs.	Brittle
Brussels Sprouts	Cut in half	6–14 hrs.	Dry, hard
Cabbage	Trim; cut in strips or grate	6–12 hrs.	Leathery, pliable
Carrots	Slice ¼" thick and steam until nearly done *or* grate and don't blanch	4–12 hrs.	Dry but slightly pliable
Cauliflower	Cut into flowerettes and pieces; steam until cooked	6–12 hrs.	Slightly pliable
Celery	Cut in strips or chop; blanching optional	6–12 hrs.	Brittle
Corn	Shuck; steam until done (5–10 mins.); trim from cob and spread on tray	4–8 hrs.	Brittle

Vegetables	*(All veggies dry at 130°F)*		
Eggplant	Peeling optional; slice ¼"–⅜" thick	6–15 hrs.	Leathery, pliable
Greens	Trim; wash; steam until wilted	3–8 hrs.	Brittle
Mushrooms	Clean or wash; slice in half or in ½" slices	4–8 hrs.	Slightly pliable; tricky to test; check for mold now and then
Onions	Trim ends; peel; slice ¼"–⅜" thick; crumble when dry	6–12 hrs.	Brittle
Peas	Shell; wash; steam until they start to pucker	6–12 hrs.	Hard
Peppers	Core; wash; slice in rings or strips, or chop	6–12 hrs.	Slightly pliable
Hot Peppers	Wash; do not blanch; dry whole	6–12 hrs.	Leathery
Potatoes	Don't peel; slice ¼" thick; steam until translucent; rinse off starch in cold water	8–12 hrs.	Brittle; tricky to test
Squash	Cook until tender; blend for leather, or chop	6–16 hrs.	Leathery or brittle
Tomatoes	Wash; dip in boiling water to loosen skin, then remove skin (optional); slice ¼"–⅜" thick	8–16 hrs.	Leathery
Zucchini	Wash; slice ¼"–⅜" thick, or grate	4–12 hrs.	Leathery

Meat, Fish, Eggs	*(Dry at 140°–145°F)*		
Beef	Cook until tender/med. rare; slice ¼"–⅜" thick, or cube	8–12 hrs.	Brittle

Meat, Fish, Eggs   (Dry at 140°–145°F)

Canned Tuna/Salmon (water-packed)	Spread on solid tray	5–12 hrs.	Flaky, dry
Eggs	Beat; add spices if desired; pour raw on solid trays	12–20 hrs.	Crumbly, dry
Fish	Clean; cut in ¼"–⅜" strips	8–15 hrs.	Brittle
Game	Cook until tender/med. rare; slice ¼"–⅜" thick, or cube	8–12 hrs.	Brittle
Poultry	Cook until done; cube, slice, or grind	8–15 hrs.	Brittle, flaky

Herbs and Spices

All	Wash; chop or dry whole	105°–110°F	Brittle; crumbly

Miscellaneous

Cheeses	Grate	140°F 4–10 hrs.	Brittle
Dry Beans	Soak; cook until tender; rinse; mash or dry whole	135°F 3–10 hrs.	Brittle, hard
Hummus	Spread ¼"–½" thick on solid tray	130°F 8–20 hrs.	Crumbly, dry
Pasta	Cook; rinse; separate well on tray	135°F 2–6 hrs.	Brittle, hard
Refried Beans	Spread ¼"–½" thick on solid tray	135°F 6–15 hrs.	Crumbly
Rice	Cook; spread in thin layer	135°F 2–6 hrs.	Hard
Salsa	Pour evenly on solid tray	135°F 12–16 hrs.	Slightly pliable, no moisture
Tofu	Cut in strips or 1" cubes; marinate if desired	130°F 6–15 hrs.	Hard or slightly pliable
Tomato sauce	Puree smooth; pour on solid tray	135°F 12–20 hrs.	Crisp to slightly pliable

Cooking Tips and Recipes

Every two weeks we walk or hitch a ride to a nearby town along the Appalachian Trail to get our food resupply. The boxes wait in the dusty back rooms of post offices, laden with dried produce, staples, trail mix; fuel that powers us north on a spine of ancient mountains wrinkled along 2,000 miles of North America.

The first time or two in town we celebrated the break in wilderness routine, the reprieve from twenty-mile days, heavy packs, and spring rains. Hot showers, dinner at a smorgasbord restaurant, a motel room with television. Luxury.

Only, after a month or more on the trail the revelry is a little forced. Once back on the ridges it takes two days to burn the glut of food out of our systems. Time and again there is nothing worth watching on television. Showers are nice, but we can wash in creeks along the way.

Georgia, North Carolina, Tennessee, Virginia. Week by week the mountain

> *ranges drop behind and spring forces its*
> *magic on the landscape. Increasingly, it is*
> *the town stops we try to avoid, not the trail*
> *life. We don't stay in motels anymore if we*
> *can help it. Pick up food, reorganize, call*
> *home, then escape from the traffic, the neon,*
> *the confusion of crowds. It is in the shad-*
> *owed forests, the airy ridges, the cherry-*
> *blossom valleys, that we find reprieve.*

Tips

A Word About Measurements

Recipes are full of exact-sounding quantities. A tablespoon of this, a cup and a half of that, half a teaspoon of something else. But who actually carries measuring spoons and measuring cups to the boonies? Instead, we become adept at using the palm of our cupped hand as an inexact spoon; we learn what size mound is about a teaspoon, or a tablespoon, or a pinch. It's a little variable, mind you, but that makes every meal just a tad different from the last time. We know, too, that a 1-quart water bottle holds 4 cups of liquid, and we've measured the capacity of our camp cup and bowl to help gauge quantities. Some of my friends use a plastic measuring cup as their wilderness mug, so that it can do double duty, but the less exact techniques are more fun.

The Veggie Mix

Many meals call for a variety of vegetables. Lentil stew, curried rice and vegetables, chili, and soups are all good with a medley of assorted produce. Over the months before a trip I dry everything from asparagus to zucchini; then I store each in its own little bag. When I get a good variety and quantity, I dump the entire assortment together and mix it up in a bucket. Then I scoop 1-cup amounts back into the bags and have a ready-mixed vegetable collage, each batch unique and primed for the backcountry stew pot.

The Fresh Touch

On shorter trips, when it isn't critical to cut every extra
ounce of weight, add a few fresh vegetables to the stock.
Carrots, onions, cauliflower, and cabbage carry well, last up
to a week in your pack, and add that flare of freshness
to a meal.

Feeding a Group

With larger groups, it's a good practice to pool ideas and
share responsibility for organizing the trip menu. Even if
one or two people are handling the food, they should solicit
suggestions from trip members for favorite meals or food
that is out of favor. The menu planners also should find out
about vegetarian preferences or food allergies *before* leaving
civilization behind.

You can get some great new meal ideas, and spread
around the responsibility for trip food, by asking each per-
son or couple to provide one dinner for the entire group.

On several trips we've told everyone to bring a surprise
food treat that costs less than five dollars, which can be
unveiled to boost spirits at some low-morale point on the
journey.

Vitamin Supplements

On trips that last longer than a month, take a supply of
multiple vitamin tablets. Your body will be demanding
more nourishment than it does at home, and it's more difficult to consistently supply a balanced blend of vitamins
and minerals on a wilderness diet. Even if you don't strictly
need them, the extra dose won't hurt.

Quick-cooking, Nutritious Staples

I remember more than one disgruntled camp scene, with
a group of famished comrades all waiting for some long-
simmering pot of food. The stars come out while pinto
beans, brown rice, or split peas cook on interminably. If
your camp is at high altitude, where things take even
longer to cook, you might as well give it up and go to bed.

Over the years I've found several shortcut staples that don't compromise nutrition or taste. White basmati rice retains much of the nutrition of brown rice, but cooks in 20 minutes and has excellent flavor. Use black-eyed peas instead of pinto, kidney, or navy beans. They cook in about 30 minutes and have a hearty nutty taste. Lentils also cook up in half an hour or less. Cracked wheat (bulgur) cooks faster than rice and makes for a nice grain option. Millet and couscous are also very fast and can be used in everything from cereals to bannock to dinners.

I like vegetable-based pastas (spinach, artichoke, veggie spirals, etc.), not because they cook faster, but because their taste and food value is superior to that of white flour noodles.

(Don't forget the option of precooked, dried staples to drastically shorten prep time. See page 15.)

Rehydrating in the Field

Far and away the easiest, and most common, way to rehydrate food is to throw it in the cook pot and let it reabsorb moisture as dinner simmers. As a rule, *add 1 cup extra water for every cup of dried food*. Then, while the rice or beans cook, the veggies plump up too.

Hot water will restore dried food more quickly than cold. If you want moist fruit for your breakfast cereal, for instance, cover it with warm water and soak overnight. At breakfast I'll start salsa rehydrating with hot water in a plastic tube. By the time I want salsa with crackers and cheese, it's ready. If you want to speed the dinner process, add water to cover your precooked staples, meats, or dried veggies several hours before you cook. Ziploc bags or plastic containers with snap-on lids work well.

For many meals, you'll be rehydrating some foods while others cook. Bring back refried beans with hot water in a bowl while you prepare the ingredients for enchiladas. In another bowl, reconstitute your dried salsa. Or, while the dried hash browns simmer, soak your scrambled eggs in cold water. For Dutch oven pizza, rehydrate veggies and tomato sauce in bowls of hot water while you work on the crust.

Finding Recipes

You'll be surprised how many of your favorite home-kitchen meals can be adapted to the field. Adjust a few gourmet ingredients, dehydrate what components you can, substitute packaged sour cream mix or dried soup mix for fresh or canned, and you're off.

Browse your favorite cookbooks or magazines, even the sides of cans and boxes, for meals with ingredients that are easy to dry and reconstitute. Frequently you won't have to change a thing. Even when you do, your creations might prove better than the originals!

The All-Important Spice Kit

Spices are, simply, the mainstay of the wilderness culinary art. Salt and pepper are all well and good. The old-timers seem to have gotten along on them, but by all reports they were a pretty crusty lot. My experience is that if salt and pepper are all you take, your taste buds will soon be picketing for change. Nothing replaces basil on vegetables and rice, chili with a dash of cumin, or a roaring curry dish on a drizzly day. Fresh garlic travels well, and spices bought at a health-food store are far cheaper, and far zestier, than the supermarket offerings.

My kit includes a minimum of the following: salt, pepper, garlic (fresh and powdered), dill, chili powder, cumin, curry, oregano, basil, thyme, bay leaves, cinnamon, and nutmeg. (Cajun mix is a nice extra.)

Condiments

Another way to work variety into your daily fare, without much extra weight, is to carry an assortment of condiments. Hot mustard, dried salsa, soy sauce or tamari, Tabasco sauce. . . . None of it adds much weight, and salsa on eggs, spicy mustard with your cheese and crackers, or soy sauce on rice all perk up meals considerably.

The Pantry

Think of it as the wilderness equivalent of the walk-in pantry at your grandmother's house. It's where you go for the extra touches, as well as such essentials as oil or flour. If you want to make a spontaneous blueberry pie, you'll find the extra bags of flour and dried milk there, along with the sugar. Coffee and tea, bouillon cubes, fruit drink crystals, sour cream mix—all the things that don't fit neatly into specific meal categories, and that might be required at any time, are stashed in the pantry. You'll learn to keep it pretty close to hand. (See "The One-Week Backcountry Menu," page 71, for a list of recommended items.)

Gourmet Twists

Often, all it takes to elevate your wilderness entree from another mundane dinner to the meal that everyone remembers is a gourmet ingredient. Try specialty and gourmet grocers or the ethnic section of your local supermarket for the best selections. Here are some suggestions:

- Thai seasoning packets and canned coconut milk (often with recipe suggestions on the packages)
- dried Oriental mushrooms: moister and more pungent than the home-dried variety, they make a great addition to pesto, spaghetti sauce, curries
- dried miniature shrimp (strong and salty, so don't overdo)
- Miso soup base: use like instant soups, or as a replacement for bouillon base in soups or stews
- dried (and potent) whole chili peppers—a tiny bag goes a long way!
- dried bean curd slices—nice to add to a vegetable stir-fry
- sun-dried tomatoes (see page 69 for recipe)

Breakfast—Fuel for Working Mornings

Unless otherwise noted, amounts are based on generous portions for two working people.

Expedition Hash

1 c. bulgur	1 tsp. basil
1 dried onion	1 Tbs. cooking oil
2½ c. water	1 Tbs. soy sauce or
black pepper and	tamari
garlic powder to taste	⅕ lb. sharp Cheddar

In saucepan, add water to bulgur and onion and bring to a boil. Toss in spices and simmer until liquid is absorbed (15 minutes). Heat oil in skillet or pan and sauté bulgur mixture until it starts to brown. Right at the end, dribble on the soy or tamari and add the cheese (I like it in chunks). When the Cheddar is melted into nice tasty globs, start eating.

Variations:
* use fresh onion; sauté it slightly before adding bulgur to oil
* use dehydrated, grated cheese instead of fresh
* vary spices: oregano, cilantro, Cajun mix
* soak bulgur overnight and go immediately into the sauté phase

Huevos Con . . .

4 dried eggs	1 Tbs. oil
spices to taste*	⅕ lb. Cheddar or Swiss
1 c. cold water	cheese (cubed)

Mix eggs and spices in cold water (¼ c. per egg) and reconstitute for a few minutes, or while you prepare one of the side dishes below. Don't be dismayed by the lumpy, watery appearance. Heat oil in skillet to medium temperature. Just before frying, add cheese to eggs. They cook in a transforming flash. By the time the cheese melts, your huevos are huevoed. (Some cut-up lunch sausage is nice in the eggs, too, if you're a meat lover.)

*May be dried in advance with the eggs; dill and pepper are old standbys, but whatever you prefer.

On the Side

Hash Browns: Simmer 1 c. dried potatoes in 1 c. water until
moisture is absorbed. Salt and pepper to taste. Slurp a little
oil in the pan and sauté until browned. Then shove the
potatoes off to the side and pour the eggs in to cook.

Frijoles: Pour hot water over 1 15-oz. can dehydrated refried
beans. Keep adding dribs and drabs of water until the
beans are right for you, and let them soak for at least 10
minutes. Fry in a little oil until heated through and slightly
browned, pile to the side of the pan, and cook the eggs that
have been patiently reconstituting alongside.

Bannock: Make bannock (see recipe on page 50) the night
before to shorten prep time. Slice it in half and fry in a little
butter before cooking the eggs. Pile your cheesy eggs on top
of your buttery, toasted muffins and you're good until lunch.

It goes without saying that salsa (fresh or reconstituted)
is *muy importado* to all of the above!

Marypat's Never-Miss Granola

1 c. dried fruit (apples, apricots, peaches are all good)	1 c. sunflower seeds
	1 c. wheat germ
	½ c. sesame seeds
4 c. rolled oats	
1 c. shredded coconut	½ c. honey
1 c. chopped almonds	½ c. vegetable oil

Mix all but the last two ingredients in a large bowl. Heat
honey and oil together in saucepan until just boiling, then
pour over dried mixture and stir thoroughly. Spread on
cookie sheets and bake in oven at 350°F for 20 minutes (or
until browned and crisp), stirring frequently.

(You can use your dehydrator to "cook" granola as well.

Spread on solid trays and set the heat at 145°F. Dry until done to your liking.)

Hot and Fruity Rice Pudding

1 qt. milk (1⅓ c. powdered with 1 qt. water)

¼ c. each: dried cranberries, cherries, blueberries (or other fruit)

¾ c. uncooked white basmati rice

¼ c. (brimming) brown sugar

½ tsp. cinnamon

½ tsp. salt

Shake up instant milk in a quart water bottle and pour into saucepan. Add everything else, fruit first, as the milk starts to heat on the stove. Bring liquid just to a boil, stirring now and again, then cover and simmer very gently until all liquid is absorbed (20 to 30 minutes). Eat hot or cool.

Dried Fruit Compote

1 c. dried fruit of choice (apples/peaches/pears/rhubarb . . .)

2 c. hot water

½ c. honey or loosely packed brown sugar

½ tsp. cinnamon

½ tsp. nutmeg (optional)

dried lemon or orange peel (optional)

Soak mixture in covered pan overnight. By morning it'll be right to gobble straight or add to your cereal bowl.

Dutch Oven Kuchen

3 c. white flour

1½ c. brown sugar

1 tsp. baking powder

½ tsp. salt

½ c. oil

1⅓ c. milk

2 dried eggs rehydrated in ½ c. water

2 tsp. vanilla

1 tsp. nutmeg

dried lemon peel

2 c. dried fruit (berries are good)

¼ c. brown sugar

Mix together the first group of ingredients, then add in sequence each of the following groups. Spread in oiled 10- to 12-inch Dutch oven and bake under coals until that smell wafts up and it's browned just right (30 to 40 minutes). This is best hot, but can also be baked the night before for breakfast.

Lunch—Keep Up the Pace

Basic Bannock

½ c. (brimming) white flour	1 tsp. baking powder
½ c. (brimming) whole wheat flour	½ tsp. salt
	3 Tbs. powdered milk
	water

These are the timeless, tried-and-true ingredients for quick camp bread. We often cook ours in the evening and have a two-meal supply (for two people) made up. Mix all dry ingredients thoroughly in a bowl (better yet, mix it and bag it before you leave) and add careful dribbles of water until the dough is slightly sticky in your hands. *Beware:* it's easy to overdo the water. Form into 4 scrupulously equal patties ½ inch to 1 inch thick. Fry over medium heat in a lightly oiled skillet until browned on the outside and cooked through.

Variations:
- add different spice combinations: garlic and chives, Cajun, cinnamon, dill . . .
- mix in dehydrated grated cheese, which will melt during cooking
- experiment with different flours
- add millet, oatmeal, wheat germ, couscous . . .
- mix in any number of extra taste ingredients like raisins, onion, sunflower seeds, etc.

Magic Mediterranean Hummus

1½ c. raw garbanzo beans (chickpeas), soaked overnight, cooked until soft (1–2 hours), and drained

3 cloves fresh minced garlic

1½ tsp. salt
pinch of cayenne
dash of tamari
juice from 2 lemons
¾ c. tahini
½ c. minced parsley
½ onion (finely chopped)

Hummus is a piquant antidote to the peanut butter blues. It makes a great spread for crackers or bannock. If you have a food processor, throw everything in and zing it into a homogenous paste. If not, mash garbanzos first, then mix it all up. Spread thinly onto solid dehydrator trays and dry at 130°F until crumbly. Powder in a blender. In the field, reconstitute with warm water. Be careful to add water slowly, because a little too much leaves you with hummus soup. This recipe should make enough spread for three lunches for two people.

Variations:
- some people like more or less garlic, tamari, or tahini
- try different beans: black beans, Anasazi beans, etc.

Ann and Phil's Lentil Pâté

1 c. lentils
3–4 c. water
2 c. stir-fried veggies (carrots/peppers/ onions/mushrooms)
2 cloves fresh, minced garlic

1 tsp. basil
1 tsp. dill
½ c. cashews
    or sunflower seeds

Another nice lunch spread for bannock or crackers that will keep you out of the clutches of peanut butter overdose. Cook the lentils until tender. Meantime, stir-fry veggies with spices for a while, and then add to the lentils and continue cooking until everything is very tender. Add in the nuts or seeds and puree in a blender. Dry on trays at 135°F until all the moisture is gone (8 to 14 hours). Crumble the dried mix or powder it in the blender, then bring it back to the desired consistency on the trail with warm water.

Remember, be careful not to add one slurp of water too many!

Fruit Leather Trail Snack

2 c. pureed fruit
water or fruit juice, as required

Almost any fruit can be made into leather, but juicy varieties like oranges have too much pulp and liquid to be convenient. Apricot, apple, peach, plum, and pear all make good leathers. Fresh fruit is superior, but frozen or canned is also feasible (pour off liquid or syrup). Cook fruit (not always necessary) until soft, but not pulpy, and puree in a blender or food processor until quite smooth (add a touch of extra water or fruit juice if needed). Pour liquid evenly onto trays and dry at 130°F until leathery and devoid of moisture pockets. Peel leather away and roll up. (You can roll on a sheet of plastic wrap to avoid sticking.) Cut into handy lengths for packing/snacking, and wrap or bag in plastic. Eat on the trail as is, or reconstitute in warm water (half as much water as fruit) to make sauce (great baby food!).

Variations:
- make combination leathers, such as apple/banana; apricot/pineapple; pear/rhubarb; peach/strawberry
- add a slight amount of honey or brown sugar for a sweeter taste
- spice with cinnamon, allspice, lemon peel, ginger . . .
- garnish with coconut, granola, chopped nuts, or other treat before drying

Miss Sue's Herky Jerky

8 lb. raw, lean meat (beef round or chuck, venison, etc.)	1 Tbs. ginger
	⅔ c. brown sugar
	1 c. premade teriyaki
1 Tbs. salt	sauce
1½ Tbs. garlic powder	1 c. soy sauce or tamari
1 tsp. black pepper	

Slice meat in thin strips, cutting across the grain. (Slightly frozen meat is easier to cut thin.) Mix all other ingredients in a large bowl, add meat, and marinate in the refrigerator at least overnight. (A plastic bowl with snap-on lid is convenient, because you can shake it to make sure all the meat is thoroughly soaked.) Dry at 140°F until done (if pieces break when you bend them, they're ready). Eat as is or cook in eggs, stews, and chilis, but ration yourself, or it'll disappear before you know it. (Makes roughly 2 pounds jerky.)

Lemony Jerky I

2 Tbs. fresh lemon juice	¼ tsp. black pepper
¼ c. olive oil	
1 tsp. salt	1 lb. meat (sliced)

Mix first four ingredients. Add meat, cover, and refrigerate 2 to 4 hours before drying.

Lemony Jerky II

1 c. pineapple juice	2 cloves minced fresh garlic
2 tsp. soy or tamari sauce	
2 tsp. fresh lemon juice	1 lb. meat (sliced)

Mix first four ingredients. Add meat, cover, and refrigerate 2 to 4 hours before drying.

Other Jerkies I Have Known

Beef and game are the standard jerky fare, but don't stop there. Some other options:

- Lamb (use leg or shoulder cuts).
- Cooked, sliced ham (raw pork is taboo!).
- Fish: Whitefish is good dried, especially if marinated in a lemon or soy sauce first. In general, the less-oily fish dry best. Clean fish and fillet into thin strips before drying at 140°F.
- Tofu (soy bean curd that comes in blocks), cut in ¼-inch strips, marinated for an hour or two, and dried at 130°F until just slightly pliable.
- Slices of cooked turkey, marinated if you like, dried until not quite brittle.

Zesty Zucchini Chips

firm, fresh zucchini in ¼- to ⅜-inch slices
garlic salt to taste

Wash zucchini. Slice, spread onto trays, and sprinkle with garlic salt. Dry at 130°F until brittle. Gobble at your leisure, but take an extra bag, because the first one will be gone by the time you get to the trailhead.

Variations:
* Cajun spices
* tamari, barbecue sauce, or mustard sauce pre-dip
* dill
* salt and vinegar

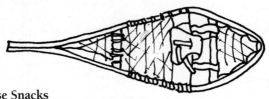

Cheese Snacks

sharp Cheddar, grated
garlic salt (or other spice) to taste

Spread grated cheese on solid tray, sprinkle spice on top, and dry at 140°F until brittle. (Without spices, this can be used in recipes that call for cheese.)

Fruit Energy Bars

1 c. vegetable oil
1 packed c. brown sugar
1 fresh egg
1 c. milk
2 Tbs. vanilla
2 tsp. cinnamon
1 tsp. nutmeg
½ tsp. powdered ginger

2 c. flour (whole wheat/
white blend)
1 tsp. baking soda

2 c. dried fruit pieces
(apricots/apples/
peaches blend
is a winner)
1 c. chopped walnuts

3 c. rolled oats
1 c. wheat germ

chocolate chips
(optional)

Mix together first group of ingredients. In order, add each remaining group. Spoon dough evenly onto baking sheet or shallow pan (12 inches by 18 inches). Bake at 350°F until browned (20 to 30 minutes). When cool, cut into trail bars.

Soups and Stews—The Simmering Pot

Soup Bases

Pretty well any soups can be cooked at home, pureed in a blender or food processor, then dried and powdered. In the field they come back in a flash with boiling water.

Lentil, black bean, and split pea are all nice this way, or used as a base in other stews. Dried cream of asparagus, broccoli, or cauliflower soups provide comforting interludes on the drizzly, cold days of a trip.

Winter squash (acorn, butternut, etc.) are good baked, peeled, and pureed with a little water. Dried and powdered they make a great starter base to which to add dried veggies and spices.

Corn Chowder

4 c. water
1 dried onion
¼ c. dried celery
1 dried green pepper
1 c. dried corn
salt to taste
plenty of black pepper
large pinches of thyme and dill
½ tsp. basil
1 chicken or vegetable bouillon cube

⅔ c. dried milk powder
2 Tbs. butter or margarine

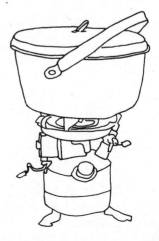

Put dried veggies in water and bring to a boil. Simmer 5 minutes, then add spices and bouillon. Keep simmering until veggies are tender. Add water if necessary. Finally, dollop on the butter and powdered milk, then turn heat way down so the pot barely bubbles, stirring to blend and cook in the flavors.

Variations:
- toasted bannock goes along nicely
- if you can tote the extra weight, replace the dried milk with a can of evaporated milk for an extra-rich texture

Barley/Mushroom Medley

6–7 c. water	1 tsp. dill
1 cube vegetable bouillon	pinch of pepper
½ c. raw barley	2 cloves minced fresh
½ c. dried mushrooms	garlic
1–2 dried onions	generous spoonful butter
2 Tbs. tamari or soy sauce	or margarine
1 tsp. salt	

This soup takes an hour or so, but if you have time and fuel, it's a hearty dinner entree. Bring water to a boil with bouillon, barley, and dried veggies. Simmer 30 minutes or so, until barley starts to plump up. Add tamari and spices and keep simmering until barley is tender, adding water if necessary. Spoon in butter for the last little bit of cooking time. (Precooked and predried barley would hasten this soup to your bowl.)

Potato-Onion Soup

6 c. water	salt and pepper to taste
1 vegetable or chicken	1 tsp. basil
bouillon cube	1 Tbs. butter
1½ c. dried potatoes	or margarine
¼ c. dried celery	⅔ c. dried milk powder
¼ c. dried carrots	1 fresh onion, chopped

The fresh onion makes this recipe, although dried onion works too. Boil dried veggies in water and bouillon for 15 to 20 minutes, or until nearly tender. Add spices, butter, milk, and onion. Continue simmering over very low heat until onion is tender and all is an evocative, savory blend.

Rainy Day Chicken/Vegetable/Noodle

6–8 c. water
2 chicken bouillon cubes
1 c. dried veggie mix
1 tsp. dried parsley
1 tsp. salt
½ tsp. basil

pepper to taste
2 5-oz. cans chicken
  (or equivalent dried)
2 c. flat or spaghetti
  noodles

Bring water to boil with all ingredients except chicken and noodles. (If using dried chicken, add at beginning.) When veggies are tender, add chicken (drained) and noodles (and more water if necessary). Cook until noodles are noodled.

Easy Lentil Stew

6 c. water
1 c. lentils
1 c. dried veggie mix
1 dried onion
1 beef bouillon cube

garlic and pepper to taste
soy sauce or tamari
  to taste
⅓ lb. sharp Cheddar,
  cubed

Add lentils and veggies to water and bring to a boil. Simmer for 30 minutes, until lentils are tender. Add water if necessary. While the pot bubbles, stir in all remaining ingredients except cheese. Just before eating, add cheese and let it melt in. (Or you can put cheese in people's bowls so the pot is easier to clean.)

Trail Chili

6–8 c. water
1 c. raw black-eyed peas
1 c. dried veggie mix
1 4-oz. can dried
  green chilis
½ c. sun-dried tomatoes
  (or regular dried)
1 dried onion
1 tsp. cumin

1 tsp. basil
1 clove fresh garlic
  (or powder to taste)
1 tsp. salt
1 Tbs. chili powder
  (or to taste)
pinch cayenne
3 Tbs. dried tomato sauce

Cook peas and dried veggies in boiling water for 20 minutes, or until peas start to soften. Add everything else, stirring, and cook until peas are tender, adding more water if necessary. Adjust seasoning to taste.

Variations:
- sprinkle with grated Parmesan or Monterey jack cheese
- add dried, cubed tofu, dried hamburger, stew meat, or crumbled jerky to cook with veggies
- garnish with sour cream from a packaged mix

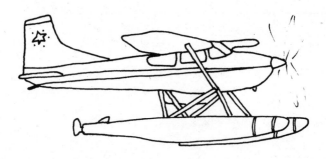

Dinner—The Day's Reward

Field-tested Pizza

3–4 c. water	1 dried pepper
½ recipe dried All-Around Tomato Sauce (page 67) or 2 15-oz. cans dried tomato sauce with Italian spices	1 dried onion
	1 bannock mix (page 50)
	warm water
½ c. dried mushrooms	⅓ lb. mozzarella cheese, thinly sliced

Boil 3 to 4 c. water in a saucepan and use to rehydrate the tomato sauce in one bowl (enough water for a fairly thick paste), and the veggies in another.

Mix dribbles of warm water with the bannock mix until

it's slightly sticky. Flatten dough evenly in the bottom of a 10- to 12-inch-diameter, lightly oiled pan (Dutch oven or heavy-gauge metal). Cook one side of dough over low heat until just barely browned, then turn uncooked side down and remove from heat.

Make an artistic layer with half of the mozzarella, pour on the sauce, then sprinkle on the drained veggies so that everyone gets the exact same goodies on each piece. Finally, add the rest of the mozzarella.

If you're cooking with fire and Dutch oven, scrape coals out of fire pit and place Dutch oven on the bare, hot ground (a very thin coal layer is okay). Use a trowel to heap hot coals on the lid and let it bake until your site smells like a pizzeria. To cook on a stove, set at very low flame, brown both sides of the crust first, cover, and check until it looks done. (A little sprinkling of water dashed on can help steam the pizza.)

Variations:
- toppings of your choice: black olives, pineapple, sliced sausage, etc., etc., etc.

Real Men Eat Dutch Oven Quiche

1 c. dried veggies of choice (zucchini/onion/carrot/tomato)

enough warm water to rehydrate (about 2 c.)

1 bannock mix (page 50)

3 Tbs. water

½ c. butter/margarine/oil (butter is best, but whatever you have in supply will work)

4 dried eggs reconstituted in 1 c. water

1½ c. milk

2 Tbs. flour

1 tsp. dry mustard

salt and pepper to taste

1 clove minced fresh garlic

½ tsp. tarragon

½ lb. cheese (Swiss/Cheddar mix is good)

paprika

Okay men, start rehydrating your veggies on the side while you tackle the crust. Mix the bannock mix, water, and butter/margarine/oil until the dough is just slightly sticky. Oil the bottom of a 10- to 12-inch-diameter Dutch oven, and press out the crust evenly with your fingers. (A smooth-sided cup makes a nice rolling pin.) Set aside.

Next, mix the eggs, milk, flour, and spices (except paprika) in a bowl and let sit.

Slice half the cheese thinly and spread over the crust. When veggies are tender, drain excess water and spread atop the cheese. Pour the liquid filling evenly over veggies. Slice the rest of the cheese and lay it decoratively over all. Finish off with a sprinkling of paprika.

Bake under coals for 30 to 45 minutes, or until you smell that baked crust. When quiche is done it will barely jiggle. If it still dances, bake some more.

Variations:

- sun-dried tomatoes or dried Oriental mushrooms are great quiche ingredients
- dill is another quichey spice, and either parsley or cilantro makes a tasty addition

One More Time Mac 'n' Cheese

3 Tbs. dried tomato sauce	1 Tbs. oil
1 tsp. dill	4 c. veggie spiral noodles
salt and pepper to taste	$\frac{1}{3}$ c. dried milk
2 qt. water	$\frac{1}{3}$ lb. Cheddar, cubed
1 dried onion	3 Tbs. margarine
$\frac{1}{2}$ c. dried peas	

Other meals you may tire of, but this old standby will keep making the menu list, trip after trip. Start by reconstituting the tomato sauce with just enough water to make a paste, along with the spices. Meanwhile, boil the onion and peas in the water until peas are nearly cooked. Add oil and noodles, and stir. When noodles are *al dente,* drain most of the water (leaving

enough to mix in milk). Return to low heat and add sauce, milk, cheese, and margarine. Stir frequently until ingredients are well mixed and cheese is melted.

Curried Rice and Veggies

3½ c. water
1 c. dried veggie mix
1 c. white basmati rice
3–4 Tbs. margarine
½ c. chopped almonds
  or cashews
½ c. raisins
2 Tbs. curry powder
  (or to taste)

Boil water and veggie mix for 5 to 10 minutes, then add rice and cover. Simmer until rice is cooked, veggies are tender, and water is pretty well gone (15 to 20 minutes). When the rice is getting close, melt margarine in large frypan or Dutch oven and sauté nuts and raisins, adding curry and stirring so that everything is coated nicely. Finally, add rice and veggies to curry and stir up together for a few minutes.

Cheesy, Spicy Beans and Ricey

4 c. water
½ c. black-eyed peas
1 4-oz. can dried
  green chilis
1 dried onion
1 c. white basmati rice
4 Tbs. dried salsa,
  rehydrated in 1 c.warm
  water
3 cloves minced fresh garlic
  (or powder to taste)
1 tsp. salt
pinch cumin
1 package sour cream mix
½ lb. Monterey jack,
  cubed

Boil water and cook peas, chilis, and onion until peas start to soften (20 minutes). Add rice, cover, and simmer until done (another 15 minutes). Drain any excess water. Meantime, rehydrate salsa with minced garlic and other spices, and mix the sour cream package up in a cup. When the rice is done, mix everything (except sour cream) together and bake briefly (if using fire), or heat on low flame until cheese melts and spices meld. Garnish with sour cream.

Spaghetti Night!

½ recipe dried All-Around Tomato Sauce (page 67), or 2 15-oz. cans dried tomato sauce simmered with Italian spices
1 c. dried veggie mix

6–8 c. water
1 tsp. oil or margarine
½ lb. spaghetti noodles (spinach or artichoke pasta is nice)
½ c. grated Parmesan cheese (optional)

Rehydrate sauce, adding boiling water until it's right for you, and simmer until the taste is perfect (more spices if necessary). Add dried veggies and extra water. While the sauce bubbles, boil 6 to 8 c. water in large pot, add oil and pasta and stir a few times. When pasta is done (10 minutes), drain and mix in the sauce. Sprinkle liberally with Parmesan and serve.

Variations:
* try garlic/parsley ribbon noodles for variety

Mushroom/Cauliflower Hot Dish

4–5 c. water
⅓ c. dried mushrooms
1 small head dried cauliflower
1 large dried onion
1 c. white basmati rice
2 cloves garlic, minced

1 tsp. basil
1 Tbs. ground lemon rind (optional)
salt and pepper to taste
⅓ lb. Cheddar, cubed small

Bring 4 to 5 c. water to a boil with the dried veggies. Simmer 10 minutes, then add rice and cover. When rice is cooked, pour off any excess water and add the remaining ingredients. Heat long enough to melt cheese and blend spices, or bake 15 minutes in Dutch oven.

Chuck's Pesto Fiesta

6–8 c. water
½ lb. spaghetti noodles
   or 4 c. veggie spirals
¼ c. olive oil
2 Tbs. melted butter
½ c. sun-dried tomatoes
½ c. Oriental dried
   mushrooms

½ dried pesto recipe
   (page 68) (packaged
   dried pesto can be
   bought at gourmet
   grocers)
¼ c. water
grated Parmesan cheese
   (optional)

Boil 6 to 8 c. water and start the noodles. At the same time, heat the oil and butter in a large pan and add tomatoes and mushrooms to sauté a bit. Then add the dried pesto powder (let the dried pesto rehydrate for several minutes in a ¼ cup of water) and sauté until it thickens nicely. Right about now the noodles will be done, so drain the water off and stir in the pesto and veggies. Serve right away, and pass the Parmesan, please.

Ah-Hoooaa! Enchilada Bake

1 large onion, dried
1 10-oz. package frozen,
   chopped spinach, dried
3 cloves minced fresh
   garlic

12 small corn tortillas
8 oz. cottage cheese
½ lb. Monterey jack,
   sliced thin

1 10-oz. can enchilada sauce (can be dried
   and then rehydrated in the field)

Heat water and rehydrate onion and spinach with the garlic (and enchilada sauce in another bowl, if necessary). Briefly fry both sides of the tortillas in a lightly oiled pan and set aside. Mix cottage cheese with rehydrated spinach mix.

To assemble, start with a small amount of enchilada sauce on the bottom of a Dutch oven or heavy pot. Then alternate layers of tortilla, cottage cheese/spinach, and

Monterey jack until you use it all up. Finish by pouring enchilada sauce evenly over the top. Any extra cheese can be sprinkled on.

Simmer over very low heat (or, better yet, bake under coals) until it's bubbly, melted, and ready to assault the taste buds.

Variations:
- black olives are nice in the cottage cheese/spinach mix
- dried refried beans, rehydrated and spooned on between layers, make a heartier dish
- cilantro is nice

Spanish Bulgur

4–5 c. water	1 tsp. salt
1 4-oz. can dried green chilis	½ tsp. oregano
2 dried onions	½ tsp. basil
1 dried green pepper	dash of garlic
2 dried tomatoes	1 Tbs. chili powder
⅓ c. black-eyed peas	pinch of cumin
1 brimming c. bulgur	⅓ lb. Monterey jack, cubed

Boil up 4 to 5 c. water with all the dried veggies and the black-eyed peas. When peas are nearly cooked (20 to 30 minutes), add bulgur and all the spices. When all is soft, juicy, and mouthwatering, throw in the cheese and heat until it's melted in.

Five-Minute Meals

There are days, unfortunately, when the very last thing you
want to do is dawdle over a meal. Days when your teeth are
chattering with cold, days when you are utterly exhausted,
days when daylight is long gone, and days when you just
aren't in the mood. You need the fuel, but would just as
soon dispatch with dinner as quickly as possible and then
go for a sunset stroll or burrow into your sleeping bag.

Many of the meals I've described already will cook in
half an hour or less, but even that can be too long. Here are
some ideas for the backcountry equivalent to calling for
take-out.

Precooked Home-cooked

The best of both worlds. Cook up some hearty dinners
before you leave home, dehydrate them, then bring them
back on the trail. Beef stew, lentil soup, chili . . . all in a
flash.

In order to speed prep time, cover the dehydrated dinner with water and seal in a Ziploc bag or snap-lid plastic
container for several hours before meal time. Add more
water as necessary. When it's time to eat, simmer for five
minutes and that's it.

I've found that the servings tend to shrink some between
the kitchen and the backcountry. (Either that or my
appetite swells.) Whatever the case, be generous with the
portions when you make precooked home-cooked meals.

Breakfast for Dinner

Just like those nights at home when a batch of scrambled
eggs suffices for supper, you can make one of the huevos
recipes from the breakfast menu and call it dinner.

Field Burritos

precooked beans (page 15) or dried refried beans from a can	dried "Salsa Supremo" (page 69) tortillas or taco shells

Reconstitute beans and salsa with hot water in separate

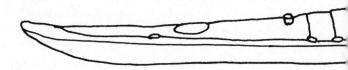

bags/containers during the day. Add water if necessary. When dinner time comes around, build your burritos or tacos and get on with the day. Grated cheese or instant sour cream mix make good additions. If you have time to cook a batch of rice (or use precooked), the meal becomes hearty and the proteins complete. (For hot burritos, warm the beans first.)

Ramen Veggies

4–5 c. water	spices of choice
1 c. dried veggie mix	½ c. grated Parmesan
Ramen noodles	cheese

For this one-pot quickie, use a veggie mixture that will reconstitute readily (green beans, zucchini, green peppers, onions, tomatoes, etc.). Bring 4 to 5 c. water to a boil with the veggies, simmer for 2 minutes, then add the noodles and spices. In 3 more minutes you'll be eating. Take a moment to sprinkle on Parmesan. (You can start veggies rehydrating during the day, if you think of it.)

Precooked Staples

See page 15 for information on precooking rice, pasta, and beans. Used in the recipes that call for them (Mac 'n' cheese, spaghetti, beans and rice, etc.), and soaked in water beforehand, they cut cooking times to the quick!

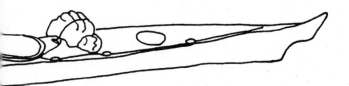

Miscellaneous Stuff that Doesn't Fit Elsewhere

Baby Food

Dehydrators are perfect for preparing nutritious trail food for the toothless set. Cook up fresh vegetables or fruit, puree, and dry on solid trays. Instant baby gruel on the trail!

Other options:
- Rehydrated fruit leather applesauce is always a hit.
- Bananas dried the long way in strips are tasty teething devices, as long as you watch to make sure they don't get swallowed whole.
- Small, hand-operated food mills are easy to pack along. Whatever mom and dad have for dinner can be ground up and spooned into that waiting open mouth.

All-Around Tomato Sauce

3 Tbs. olive oil
1 large onion, chopped
3 cloves fresh garlic, minced
1 large green pepper
2 tsp. basil
1 tsp. oregano
1 bay leaf
2 tsp. salt

2 15-oz. cans tomato sauce
1 6-oz. can tomato paste
1 Tbs. red wine
2 fresh tomatoes, chopped
½ tsp. black pepper

Sauté the first group of ingredients, then add the second group and simmer over low heat for an hour or more. Spread on solid trays (puree first, if you like), and dry at 135°F until crisp. Peel off, break up in small pieces, or powder in a blender. This recipe makes enough sauce for two dinners (spaghetti, pizza, etc.).

Variations:
- at the end of cooking, add a handful of chopped parsley
- use additional veggies in initial sauté (mushroom, celery, carrot)
- add ground beef or ½ lb. cubed tofu to the first sauté

Pesto

3 c. (tightly packed) fresh
    basil leaves, in pieces
½ c. chopped walnuts
3 cloves minced garlic
½ tsp. salt
¾ c. grated Parmesan
    cheese

½ c. chopped parsley
plenty of ground black
    pepper
¾ c. olive oil/melted butter
    blend (½ c. oil to ¼ c.
    butter is pretty
    standard)

You can buy premade dried pesto, but homemade, as usual, is better. The tough part is blending all the dry ingredients into a paste. A food processor works best, but a blender will do. Mix all the dry ingredients and blend slowly (a little water may be required) into a coarse paste. Spread on trays and dry gently (125°F or so) until crumbly. Powder thoroughly in a blender. In the field, melt butter and oil together and mix powder in slowly until it gels into a thick, homogeneous paste. (Makes enough pesto for two generous dinners for two.)

Variations:
- try almonds, cashews, or pine nuts instead of walnuts
- cilantro mixed with the parsley makes for a distinctive taste variation

Salsa Supremo

1 large onion	1 Tbs. chili powder
3 cloves minced fresh garlic	3 c. chopped tomatoes (or 2 15-oz. cans)
2 Tbs. olive oil	1 4-oz. can dried green chilis
½ tsp. salt	1 c. water
½ tsp. cumin	¼ c. hearty red wine
½ tsp. cayenne (or to taste)	1 3-oz. tomato paste

Again, you can go store bought, but why? Heat up the oil in a nice heavy skillet and sauté the onion and garlic. Add all the spices, using only the amount of cayenne that suits you, and sauté a minute longer. Now add all the rest, turn down the temperature, and simmer a good long time—at least an hour—adding water if necessary.

Puree in a blender and dry on solid trays like the tomato sauce. Break into small pieces or powder in a blender. On the trail, rehydrate with hot water in a screw-top container or plastic food tube. Keep it handy for eggs, crackers and cheese, or to add that extra zing to dinners . . . it's habit forming. (Makes about 4 c.)

Sun-dried Tomatoes

Use firm ripe plum tomatoes. After washing, cut in half lengthwise and remove cores. Arrange skinside down on trays with ample space between

tomatoes. Dry at 135 to 140°F for 10 to 20 hours. When done, tomatoes will be leathery, but free of moisture pockets or tacky spots.

You can store sun-dried tomatoes like any other produce, or pack them in jars of olive oil with garlic and herbs. Kept in olive oil, tomatoes can be used as is. If packed dry, let them plump up in hot water for 10 minutes before cooking with them.

Pizza, pesto, pasta dishes, and quiche are all greatly enhanced by sun-dried tomatoes. Their pungent, earthy flavor and wonderful chewy texture lend a gourmet touch to meals cooked far from home.

The One-Week Backcountry Menu

Eli is only eight months old. He seems tiny and vulnerable when I lay him in the bow of the canoe. It is the first morning of his first expedition, and I am more nervous now than I ever have been before running a big rapid, more nervous than on the first day of a year-long wilderness journey. We will spend a month traveling nearly 600 miles of the Yellowstone River through Montana. It doesn't help my confidence that he is complaining loudly as we shove off. What are we doing, anyway? But half a mile downstream he is blissfully asleep, lulled by the jostling current, his chubby slumbering face shaded by a colorful sun hat.

Many wilderness diets are predicated, it seems to me, on the premise that you can survive on anything, provided you don't have to do it for long. The predictable results are terminal gastronomic boredom, group morale that begins to plummet soon after the first lunch, and the myriad consequences (some potentially serious) of insufficient nutrition.

In the boonies your food needs to have variety, taste, and solid nutrition. Flexibility is important too—the ability to adapt to changing weather, fatigue, and the whims of the moment.

An active outdoor life can require 3,000 to 6,000 calories a day just to metabolically tread water. Throw in a chilling rain, an unplanned dunking on a river crossing, or a steep pass or two to hike over, and the caloric demands go even higher. It's not the time to make do on meager rations with the nutritional value of cardboard.

Group morale plays a critical role in the success of a trip, a role that is often underestimated—until you live through a journey full of bickering and tension, that is. And believe me, nothing erodes good nature more quickly than a monotonous, scanty diet. When that plaintive wail rises up, "Instant oatmeal *again*?" or "Aren't there any seconds?", you know you're in for a long haul.

I remember a couple of guys I met on a trip in northern Quebec. Their food wasn't bad, although three times heavier than necessary. Problem was, they had given themselves the same few meals over and over. By the time I met them, they'd endured this monotony for several weeks already. Hungry or not, after a few bites they threw most of their food into the fire. And all they seemed able to talk about was the gourmet fare they'd eat when they got back home.

Beyond all that, it's pure fun to ad lib. Say you reward yourself with a rest day after a week of tough slogging. Say there's a big patch of ripe blueberries loading the bushes near camp. Wouldn't it be a treat to throw together a fresh blueberry pie? Or, another time, when you decide you're tired of the rice dish that has already come around once. . . . No prob! Make a curry sauce to go over it, or a cheese sauce. Or, for that matter, skip the rice meal altogether and make broccoli quiche instead!

The One-Week Menu

Note the emphasis on variety in the food plan that follows. No dinner is repeated. Although you have eggs for breakfast twice, once it's with potatoes, the next time with refried beans. Lunch trail mix is salty one day, sweet another. The cheeses vary. Condiments from the pantry can be employed at any time to increase taste options.

These meals can all be cooked either on a stove or over a fire. With a minimum of effort you can add three more dinners to make a 10-meal rotation. Even on a trip that lasts months, you won't repeat dinners more than a handful of times. Most of us hardly do better than that at home!

Also, several dinners are quick to prepare, a merciful benefit when a rainstorm is brewing or you don't camp until after dark. The macaroni and cheese, curried rice, or lentil stew can all be finished in 30 minutes. For even faster meal ideas, see page 65. For specific cooking directions, see the recipes, beginning on page 47.

Finally, don't underestimate the importance of an occasional treat: dessert once in a while; hard candies, chocolate, or fruit leather for an afternoon boost; a flask of whiskey for campfire evenings. . . . A four-star outing turns into five-star bliss.

Week at a Glance

Day	Breakfast	Lunch	Dinner
One	Granola	Cheese, nuts, crackers, bannock, dried fruit, peanut butter, jelly, hummus, meat spread, sausage, jerky, condiments in daily allotments (see following table)	Easy Lentil Stew

Day	Breakfast	Lunch	Dinner
Two	Expedition Hash	See page 73	Curried Rice & Veggies; Cheesecake
Three	Oatmeal		Mushroom/Cauliflower Hot Dish
Four	Huevos (Eggs) with Hash Browns		One More Time Mac 'n' Cheese
Five	Cold cereal		Spanish Bulgur
Six	Seven-Grain cereal		Trail Chili; pudding
Seven	Huevos (Eggs) with Frijoles		Spaghetti Night

Food-Pack Contents (For Two Adults)

Day	Breakfast	Lunch	Dinner
One	1⅓ c. granola; 6 Tbs. powdered milk	RyKrisp crackers; ¼ lb. Swiss; ⅓ lb. salty nut mix; 2 dried apples; 4 strips jerky	1 c. lentils; 1 dried onion; 1 c. dried veggie mix; ⅕ lb. Cheddar; 1 beef bouillon cube
Two	1 c. bulgur; 1 dried onion; ⅕ lb. Cheddar	2 bannock rolls; 1 can meat spread; 2 dried bananas; ⅓ lb. sweet nut mix	1 c. dried veggie mix; 1 c. white basmati rice; ½ c. chopped almonds or cashews; ½ c. raisins; instant cheesecake mix
Three	2 servings oatmeal; ⅓ c. raisins; 4 Tbs.	2 bannock rolls; dried hummus (¾ c. wet); ⅓ lb.	⅓ c. dried mushroom; 1 small head dried cauliflower;

Day	Breakfast	Lunch	Dinner
	powdered milk	sesame nut mix; 2 dried peaches; 4 jerky strips	1 large dried onion; 1 c. white basmati rice; ⅓ lb. Cheddar
Four	4 dried eggs; 1 dried green pepper; ⅕ lb. Swiss; 1 c. dried potatoes	club crackers; ¼ lb. Monterey jack; ⅓ lb. salty nut mix; 4 dried apricots	3 Tbs. dried tomato sauce; 1 dried onion; ½ c. dried peas; 4 c. veggie spiral noodles; ⅓ c. powdered milk; ⅓ lb. Cheddar, cubed
Five	1½ c. cold cereal; ⅓ c. raisins or other dried fruit; 6 Tbs. powdered milk	2 bannock rolls; peanut butter (⅓ plastic camping tube); ⅓ c. jelly; ⅓ lb. sweet nut mix; 2 dried pears; salami roll (optional)	1 4-oz. can dried green chilis; 2 dried onions; 1 dried green pepper; 2 dried tomatoes; ⅓ c. black-eyed peas; 1 c. (brimming) bulgur (cracked wheat); ⅓ lb. Monterey jack
Six	2 servings 7-grain cereal; ⅓ c. raisins; 4 Tbs. powdered milk	2 bannock rolls; 1 can meat spread; ⅓ lb. salty nut mix; 2 dried apples	1 c. raw black-eyed peas; 1 c. dried veggie mix; 1 c. dried tomatoes; 1 4-oz. can dried green chilis; 1 dried onion; 3 Tbs. dried tomato crystals; instant pudding mix
Seven	4 dried eggs; ⅕ lb. Swiss; 1 c. dried refried beans	wheat crackers; ¼ lb. Cheddar; ⅓ lb. sesame nut mix; 2 dried bananas; salami (optional)	½ recipe dried All-Around Tomato Sauce; 1 c. dried veggie mix; ½ lb. spaghetti noodles; ½ c. grated Parmesan (optional)

The Pantry

1-lb. squeeze bottle margarine
1 pint cooking oil
1 c. tamari or soy sauce

dried salsa (as desired)
4 dried eggs (optional, for baking)
small bag powdered milk

tea (as desired)
coffee (as desired)
cocoa (as desired)
drink crystals (as desired)
home-dried soups
(optional, for hot
lunches)
complete spice kit
small bag brown sugar

small bag flour (optional,
for baking)
treats (hard candy/
chocolate/fruit leather/
licorice, as desired)
liquor (as desired)
desserts (pudding, instant
cheesecake, etc.)

Final Advice

Look this over closely before you pack it up verbatim, then adjust to your tastes. If you don't want to bother baking bannock, take more crackers (light, but bulky). Want more meat? Put diced salami in the eggs or dehydrate some stew beef for lentil stew or chili. If you prefer a lightning start in the morning, or plan to be in a hot climate, forget the hot cereal and increase the granola. Plan to catch fish? Replace a breakfast and a dinner or two with fish entrees. You'll quickly find ways to trim here, add there, put your own twists on meals.

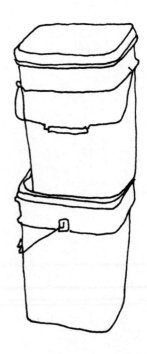

My wilderness menu is constantly changing, even in the midst of a trip. I grow tired of recipes, try new ones. On some forays I cook on fires and use a Dutch oven to make pizza, quiche, enchilada casserole. On others I go as light as possible, cook on a stove, and plan several dinners that require little or no cooking.

Some of these dinners can be prepared and dried before you leave home. Chili, spaghetti sauce, or lentil stew all come back wonderfully and quickly. If you plan to do this, make about one-third more than usual, since the drying process seems to shrink portions.

Two Easy Dehydrator Plans

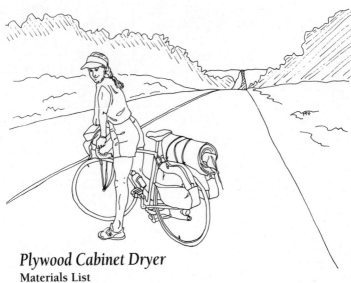

Plywood Cabinet Dryer

Materials List

Quantity	Item
4	2" x 2" x 36" corner posts (frame)
2	¾" x 12" x 20" plywood (top and bottom)
2	¼" x 12" x 37½" plywood (sides)
1	¼" x 20½" x 37½" plywood (back)
1	porcelain lamp fixture with hardware
1	150-watt bulb
18	¾" quarter-round strips in 12" lengths (guides)
9	16¼" x 10¼" metal cooling racks (drying shelves)
2	¼" x 20½" x 18¾" plywood (front, bottom and door)
2	hinges
2	door hasps
	2" drywall screws
	1½" drywall screws
	wood glue
1	oven thermometer (optional)
1	door handle (optional)
1	dimmer switch (optional)
4	metal shelving tracks 18" long, with tabs (optional, to replace wood shelf guides)

Front View

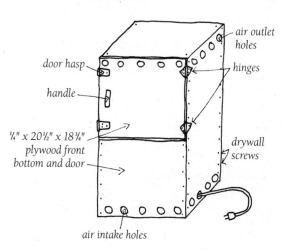

air outlet holes

door hasp

hinges

handle

¼" x 20½" x 18¾" plywood front bottom and door

drywall screws

air intake holes

Inside Front View

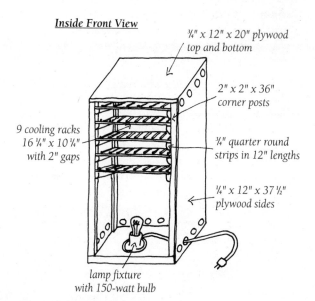

¾" x 12" x 20" plywood top and bottom

2" x 2" x 36" corner posts

9 cooling racks 16 ¼" x 10 ¼" with 2" gaps

¾" quarter round strips in 12" lengths

¼" x 12" x 37 ½" plywood sides

lamp fixture with 150-watt bulb

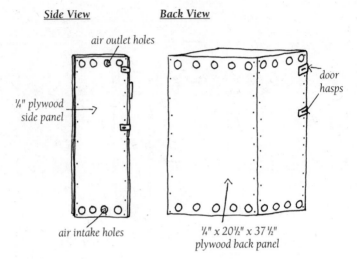

Side View   _Back View_

air outlet holes

¼" plywood
side panel

door
hasps

air intake holes   ¼" x 20½" x 37½"
plywood back panel

Building Instructions

1. Use 2" drywall screws to fasten the top and bottom ¾"
   plywood to the 2" x 2" frame. Make the 2" x 2" corners
   flush under the ¾" plywood.
2. With wood glue and 1½" drywall screws, fit the ¼"
   plywood sides and back to the box.
3. Drill rows of ¾" holes at top and bottom of the box all
   around. (These are your air circulation intake and outlet
   holes.)
4. Mount the porcelain lamp fixture in the center of the
   bottom and run the cord out through one of the vent
   holes.
5. Screw the 18 strips of ¾" quarter-round (shelf guides),
   flat side up, into the 2" x 2" corner posts. Space them 2"
   apart in the top half of the cabinet (9 on a side). Your 16
   ½" x 10¼" metal drying racks will rest on these strips.
6. Cover the front bottom half of the cabinet with ¼"
   plywood, attached with glue and drywall screws.
7. Make your cabinet door out of ¼" plywood, 20½" x
   18¾", hinged on one side, with hasps on the other.
8. Fit a handle to the door (optional).

9. Drill a row of ¾" holes at the top and bottom of the cabinet front.
10. Screw in the 150-watt bulb to the lamp fixture.

Additional Options
- a dimmer switch on the lamp cord will allow you to adjust the heat level
- hang an oven thermometer on the back wall
- instead of using quarter-round for the shelf guides, install metal shelving tracks to the corner posts with adjustable tabs to vary the shelf spacing

Coldframe Solar Dryer
Cut sun-drying times in half by setting this simple frame over your trays.

Building Instructions
1. Paint the 4' x 6' x ¼" plywood panel black.
2. Build the simple 1" x 2" wood frame as illustrated.
3. Attach the back to the frame with 1" drywall screws.
4. Use plastic to cover front and sides, attached with staple gun, or Plexiglas attached with screws.

Front View

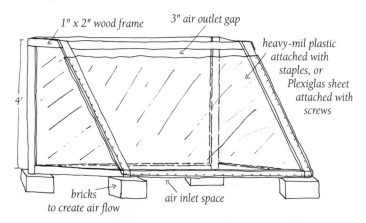

1" x 2" wood frame · 3" air outlet gap · heavy-mil plastic attached with staples, or Plexiglas sheet attached with screws · 4' · bricks to create air flow · air inlet space

<u>**Back View**</u>

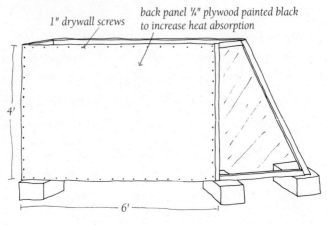

1" drywall screws

back panel ¼" plywood painted black
to increase heat absorption

4'

6'

<u>**Side View**</u>

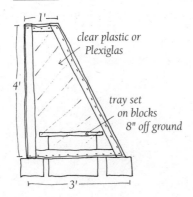

1'

4'

clear plastic or
Plexiglas

tray set
on blocks
8" off ground

3'

Index